CW01481488

Copyright © 2024 by Scott Palmer

ISBN:978-1-0881-4501-2 All rights reserved. No part of this book may be reproduced or transmitted in any form or by any means, electronic or mechanical, including photocopying, recording, or by any information storage and retrieval system, without permission from the copyright owner.

Published by Cypress Hills Press
Brooklyn, New York

Book design: Richard Tackett
https://www.facebook.
com/TackettDesign/

HOUSE OF CARDS TRILOGY: THE SERIES

BY

SCOTT PALMER

INTRODUCTION

This is a reference book on THE HOUSE OF CARDS trilogy, starring Ian Richardson, which was in three separate parts consisting of four episodes for each section. They include *House of Cards* (1990), *To Play the King* (1993), and *The Final Cut* (1995).

The book includes all three parts and twelve episodes, in original transmission date order, and includes complete cast lists, numerous photographs, directorial credits, and a story synopsis for each episode.

The political thriller *House of Cards* is comprised of four episodes, set after the end of Margaret Thatcher's tenure as Prime Minister.

The story tells the manipulative and sudden rise to power of Conservative Whip Francis Urquhart, an extreme right wing politician, frustrated over his lack of promotion and the weakness of the new government.

Thus, he plots an extremely calculated and meticulous plan to bring down the Prime Minister and replace him. During this drawn-out, ruthless coup, his life is complicated by his relationship with young female reporter Mattie Storin, whom he uses to leak sensitive information.

Andrew Davies adapted the story from the 1989 Michael Dobbs novel of the same title. *House of Cards* was said to draw from *Richard III* and *Macbeth*.

Both of these stories feature main characters who are corrupted by power and ambition. Urquhart frequently talks to the audience through the camera.

4

To Play the King is the second part of the *House of Cards* trilogy. Directed by Paul Seed, it was adapted by Andrew Davies. The series details the conflict between P.M. Francis Urquhart and a newly crowned king as well as the run-up to the general election.

The new King becomes involved in politics in a way that Urquhart finds unacceptable for a constitutional monarch.

Tensions escalate when Urquhart moves his moderate environment secretary after rejecting his proposals to regenerate inner cities.

The King's Assistant Press Secretary, Chloe Carmichael, leaks the outcome of the meeting to the press, which rankles Urquhart.

Urquhart obtains "regal insurance" from Princess Charlotte, a royal family member. Urquhart also begins regularly meeting with the King's ex-wife.

He continually assures her that he has no intention of disturbing the Monarchy, implying he would support the early accession of her teenaged son as King.

Urquhart threatens the King with Charlotte's memoirs, saying that he will be forced to publish them if the King continues to publicly oppose him.

He also blackmails newspaper man Bullerby into publishing Charlotte's memoirs in the Daily Clarion, threatening to release images of his sexual relationship with the princess.

Urquhart arranges for Corder to have the King abducted by thugs during his tour of a Manchester estate; the military was following the King on Urquhart's orders, rescuing him from possible harm. The King is seen as foolish for his negligence in the matter of security, and Urquhart seems like a hero for having protected him.

Meanwhile, Corder discovers that Stamper has passed information on Mattie Storin's murder to a journalist as insurance. With urging from his wife Elizabeth, Urquhart orders Corder to assassinate them. Their deaths are put down to the I.R.A.

The Conservatives subsequently win the general election with a 22-seat overall majority. With his policies vindicated by the electorate, despite the King's public opposition, Urquhart demands his abdication.

The new teenaged King is crowned, showing that Urquhart had succeeded in obtaining the abdication of the previous king. Urquhart grins at the camera and says "God save the King."

The Final Cut is the third part of the trilogy. Directed by Mike Vardy, the serial details the conclusion of Francis Urquhart's tenure as Prime Minister. He aims to pass the longevity tenure of the late Margaret Thatcher-which he does.

There are numerous flashbacks to the deaths of Mattie Storin as well as two young Cypriots Urquhart killed while serving as a 19-year-old army lieutenant in 1956.

On a motorway near London, Urquhart's limousine is forced off the road by a car containing three drunken louts. The attackers threaten Urquhart's party with baseball bats, but are shot dead by security staff as they approach.

Urquhart himself sustains minor head injuries in the collision, but his life is not endangered. Deputy P.M. Tom Makepeace chairs a cabinet meeting while Urquhart is in hospital.

The brother of the murdered Greek Cypriot guerrillas, who witnessed their deaths, lives in London and recognizes Urquhart as the soldier who killed them. He asks his daughter Maria to investigate.

Meanwhile, Urquhart enrages Makepeace by making a speech in the House of Commons suggesting that Britain should not adopt the Euro, but that Europe should instead adopt English as its official language. Makepeace resigns and becomes an adversary to Urquhart.

Makepeace's leadership challenge has attracted enough support to convince Urquhart that his position is in jeopardy. After a Cyprus debacle, Urquhart's support plummets; Corder tells Mrs. U. that drastic measures are needed.

Urquhart despairs, but Elizabeth consoles him. Corder has a plan: at the unveiling of the Margaret Thatcher memorial, on the day when Urquhart surpasses her record, a sniper in Corder's services appears on a rooftop and shoots the prime minister dead.

Elizabeth had arranged for his assassination as the only way to preserve his reputation (and the retirement fund). Urquhart dies in her arms, while Corder offers his services to Makepeace, the apparent successor.

Ian Richardson's most acclaimed television role was as the Machiavellian Francis Urquhart in the *House of Cards* trilogy. He won the BAFTA Best Television Actor Award for his portrayal in the first series, *House of Cards* (1990), and was nominated for both of the sequels, *To Play the King* (1993) and *The Final Cut* (1995). Andrew Davies won an Emmy award for outstanding writing in a miniseries.

TABLE OF CONTENTS:

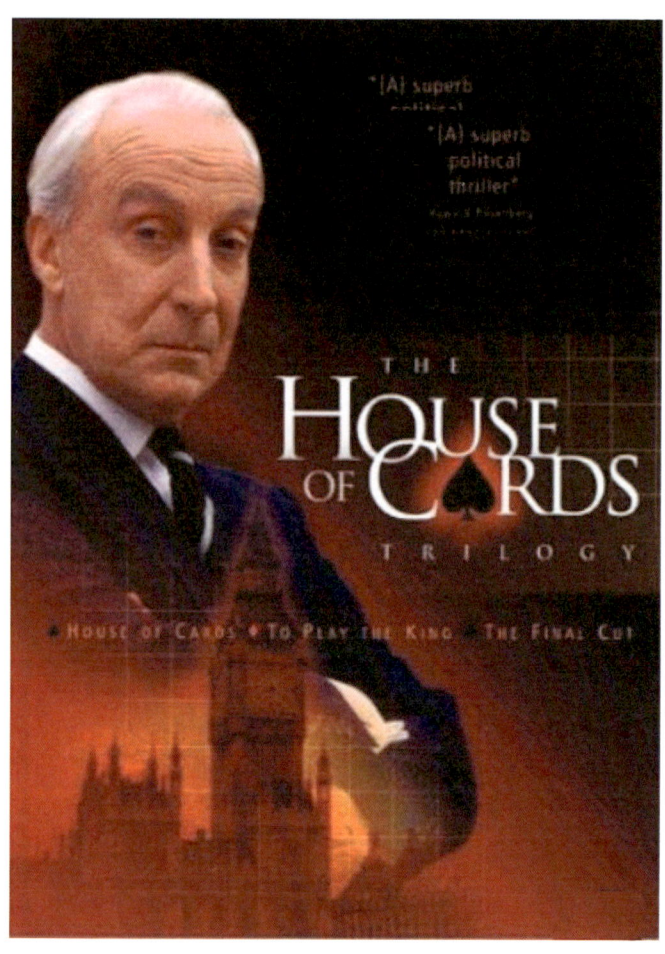

HOUSE OF CARDS EPISODE 1

DIRECTED BY Paul Seed
ORIGINAL AIR DATE: 11/18/90

CAST

Ian Richardson.........Francis Urquhart
Susannah Harker............Mattie Storin
David Lyon..P.M. Henry Collingridge
Miles Anderson............Roger O'Neill
Diane Fletcher......Elizabeth Urquhart
Malcolm Tierney.......Patrick Woolton
Kenny Ireland................Ben Landless
James Villiers.....Charles Collingridge
Colin Jeavons.................Tim Stamper
Nicholas Selby.......Lord Billsborough
Damien Thomas......Michael Samuels
Alphonsia Emmanuel........Penny Guy
William Chubb...........John Krajewski
John Hartley..............Greville Preston
Christopher Owen..............McKenzie
Kenneth Gilbert..............Harold Earle
Isabelle Amyes........Ann Collingridge
Raymond Mason........................Stoat
John Arnatt...........Sir Jasper Grainger
Robert Ashby........................Presenter
Angela Rippon.................Newsreader

Ian Richardson

Ian Richardson

Susannah Harker

David Lyon

Miles Anderson

Diane Fletcher

Malcolm Tierney

Kenny Ireland

Frank Williams......................Treasurer
Tommy Boyle.........Stephen Kendrick
Jeff Nuttall.............................Biggman
David Blake Kelly..Charles Goodman
Sally Faulkner....Junior Health Minister
Colin Dudley..........................Speaker
Henrietta Voigts...................Secretary
Tariq Yunus..........................Jhabwala
Gertan Klauber...................Blackhead
Nadim Sawalha...........Bank Manager
Michael Tomlinson.............Constable
Alex Leppard............Commissionaire
Delavel Astley........Political Secretary
Nick Brimble...........................Corder
Kevork Malikyan..............Mr. Naresh
Leslie Mills..........................Detective

James Villiers   Colin Jeavons

Nicholas Selby   Damien Thomas

Alphonsia Emmanuel   William Chubb

John Hartley   Christopher Owen

Kenneth Gilbert   Isabelle Amyes

Raymond Mason   John Arnatt

AND: Mark Abbott, Joy Adams, Liz
Adams, Nancy Adams, Steve A'Dor,
Francis Agnew, Steve Aliffe, Jack
Armstrong, Yvonne Ash, Andrea Ash-
ley, Richard Ashley, Robert Ashley-
Moore, Patricia Astley, Richard Ather-
ton, David Bache, Norman Bacon, Jon
Baker, Samantha Baker, Colin Bald-
win, Gregory Ball, Rosemary Banks,
Anthony Barratt, Kip Barrs, Ilana
Barry, Tammy Bass, Francis Batsoni,
Samantha Beale, Paul Beaumont, Ja-
son Beazley, Bernard Bennett, Alice
Benson, Barbara Bermel, Bobby Ber-
nard, Peter Bex, David Billa, Hilary
Bishop, Jane Bishop, Pete Blacker,
Nicholas Blatt, Karen Bourne, Peggy

Bourne, Andrew Bowen, Willy Bowman, Tommy Boyle, Mark Breckon, Mark Brett, Monique Briant, Michael Britton-Jones, Oliver Broome, Mike Brown, John Buckland, David Bulbeck, Jack Burns, Stephen Calcutt, Amanda Carlson, Fran Carder, Sandi Carter, Con Chambers, Ray Chaney, Jean Channon, Arnold Chazen, Johnny Clamp, Ina Clare, Ann Clarke, Melita Clarke, Micky Clarke, Trisha Clarke, Helena Clayton, David Cleeve, Lindsey Cole, Michael Cole, Mair Coleman, Judy Collins, Ken Coombs, Eric Corlett, Judy Cowne, Ron Cozzi, Pamela Craine, Robert Crake, Chris Cresswell, Alan Crisp, Bert Crome, Jennifer Crome, Cyril Crook, Avril Dean, Jim Delany, Jan Denham, Terrance Denville, John Emms, Valerie Eve, Jill Fentiman, Keith Ferrari, Peter Finn, Simon Fisher-Becker, Carole Fisher-Grant, Noel Flanagan, Christian Fletcher, Alison Ford, Ruby Fox, Sally Fox, Irene Frederic, Jack Frost, Iris Fry, Ann Gabrielle, Paul Galloway, Salo Gardner, Martin Garfield, David Garry, Helen Garton, Alec Gifford, Selena Gilbert, Vivienne Glance, Alan Gold, Jill Goldston, Jenny Goodall, Laurie Goode, Vanessa Goodwright, Pat Gorman, Paul Govas, Alan Gray, Charlie Gray, Chrissie Grech, Christina Green, Ron Gregory, Jan

Robert Ashby

Angela Rippon

Frank Williams

Tommy Boyle

Jeff Nuttall

David Blake Kelly

Sally Faulkner

Colin Dudley

Henrietta Voigts

Tariq Yunus

Gertan Klauber

Nadim Sawalha

Griffiths, Donald Groves, Dorothy Grumbar, Eldon Guller, Jean Hall, Mark Hallett, Adrian Hammond, June Hammond, Dave Hampson, Dick Harris, Gordon Harris, Paul Hart, John Hartley, Frank Harvey, Lloyd Harvey, Pearl Hawkes, Glen Hayes, Mandy Hearnden, Bill Hemmings, Carla Hendricks, Judy Herbert, Christine Hewitt, Vanessa Heywood, Kit Hillier, David Hillman, Josephine Hinchley, Freddie Hogarth, Barrie Holland, Ray Holland, Lew Hooper, Dick Hope, Clive Hopkins, Elaine Hopkins, Diane Horsey, Terri Howard, Paul Howlett, Ivor Humphris, Derek Hunt, Graham Hunter, John Huntley, Clive Hurst, Caroline Huxley, Cavid Ianson, Steve Ismay, Barbara Jaeson, Humph James, Juliette James, Lawrie James, Bernard Jamieson, Graham Jarvis, Kevin Jarvis, Ian Jason, Geraldine Jay, Simon Joseph, Paul Joy, Helen Judson, Luke Kelly, Rick Kennedy, Eric Kent, Leo Kersley, Richard King, Audrey Kirby, Mark Kirby, Paul Kirby, Harry Klein, Penny Lambirth, Ken Lawrie, Michael Leader, Pat LeClerc, Aileen Lewis, Alex Lewis, Debbie Lloyd, Peter Lloyd, Joan Lovelace, Ann Luksys, Maggie Lynton, Jay McGrath, Alison McGuire, Wyn McLeod, Ronald Markham, John Marley, Kay Marshall, Raymond Martin, Tina Maskell,

Kevork Malikyan

Leslie Mills

Ina Clare

Simon Joseph

Harry Klein

Cy Town

Cabinet Minister

House Official 1

House Official 2

M.P. 1

M.P. 2

M.P. 3

Raymond Mason, Gary Matthews, Gina Maufe, Mary Maxted, Kate Meadows, David Melbourne, Ken Mercer, Julie Michelle, Ellen Miller, Nicolle Mills, Gareth Milne, Maggie Mitchell, Peter Moore, Julie Morgan, Brian Morgan-Carter, Jo Montgomery, John J. Moore, Lola Morice, James Muir, Mike Mulloy, Fiona Murray, Gary Murray, Honor Myers, Stuart Myers, Maureen Nelson, Jacqueline Noble, Lloyd Notice, Susan Nye, Kevin O'Brien, Tony O'Leary, Marie O'Mahoney, Gabrielle Parker, Tony Parkin, Oscar Peck, David Pelton, Pat Pelton, John Perrin, Patsy Peters, Joe Phillips, Noreen Phillips, Selwyn Pitcher, Bronek Pomorski, Adam Poulton, Brychan Powell, Sheila Power, Kaye Power-McGowan, Ken Pritchard, Paul Puig, Caroline Quennell, Susan Raasay, Celia Radband, Michael Reeves, Fred Reford, Leslie Rhodes, Lee Richards, Joseph Riordan, Evan Ross, David Rowley, Philip Sadler, Nicky Sands, Ivan Santon,

Man 1   Man 2

Man 3   Reporter

Woman

John Sargent, Terry Sartain, Eddy May Scandrett, Monty Scott, Roy Seeley, Grant Shelley, Pat Shepherd, Larry Sheppard, Roland Sidwell, Sally Sinclair, Harjit Singh, Virginia Slade, Barbara Smith, Edwina Smith, Robert Smythe, Anthony Snell, Judd Solo, Sharon St. Clare, Guy Standeven, Douglas Stark, Tony Starr, Sarah Jane Stedman, Lionel Stevens, Maureen Stevens, Marcus Still, David Stowell, Yvonne Stroud, Gary Sutcliffe, Derek Suthern, Keith Swaden,

Paul Symington, Judy Szucs, Sue Tarry, Colin Thomas, Reg Thomason, Cy Town, Frank Tregear, Patricia Turton, Chris Underhill, Alan Uttley-Moore, Harry Van Engel, Derek Van Weenen, Janet Varley, Mike Vaughan, Annette Vellender, Christine Walker, Jay Watson, Jeff Wayne, Trevor Wedlock, Leslie Weekes, David Weller, Arthur Wells, Joe Wells, Joe Wenborne, Barbara Whateley, Lionel Wheeler, Eddie Whiting, Alan Wicks, Barrie Wilkinson, Elaine Williams, Llewellyn Williams, Raymond Williams, Trevor Willis, Sachaley Wilson, Stuart Windsor, Sue Winkler, Tony Winn, Tina Winter, Jana Winward, Tommy Winward, Kay Woodgate, Syd Wragg, Mavis Wright

Francis Urquhart is the Conservative Party Chief Whip who keeps the party's Members of Parliament in line. The party has selected a new leader, Henry Collingridge, and at the general election the government is returned with a reduced majority.

Ian Richardson, Malcolm Tierney

Ian Richardson outside 10 Downing Street

Miles Anderson and friend

Urquhart expects his proper reward-a senior Cabinet post-but is shocked when the Prime Minister tells him he's to stay where he is. Urquhart decides to exact his revenge. Using an ambitious young journalist, Mattie Storin, he plants rumors of dissension in the party.

When Urquhart arrives at Downing Street, Collin-gridge tells him that his memorandum is radical, but Urquhart replies that the country needs a change.

Ian Richardson, David Lyon

Ian Richardson, Colin Jeavons

Ian Richardson, Kenny Ireland

David Lyon and associate

Collingridge says that while he appreciates all of Urquhart's suggestions, they will remain suggestions rather than ministerial policies. There are to be no cabinet changes at all.

Ian Richardson, Susannah Harker

Frank Williams, Colin Jeavons

He also says that Urquarhart is the best Chief Whip the party has had since the war, and a good Chief Whip is more important than a good Home Secretary. Francis takes that with a grain of salt.

James Villiers, Kenny Ireland, Susannah Harker

Mattie at the press conference

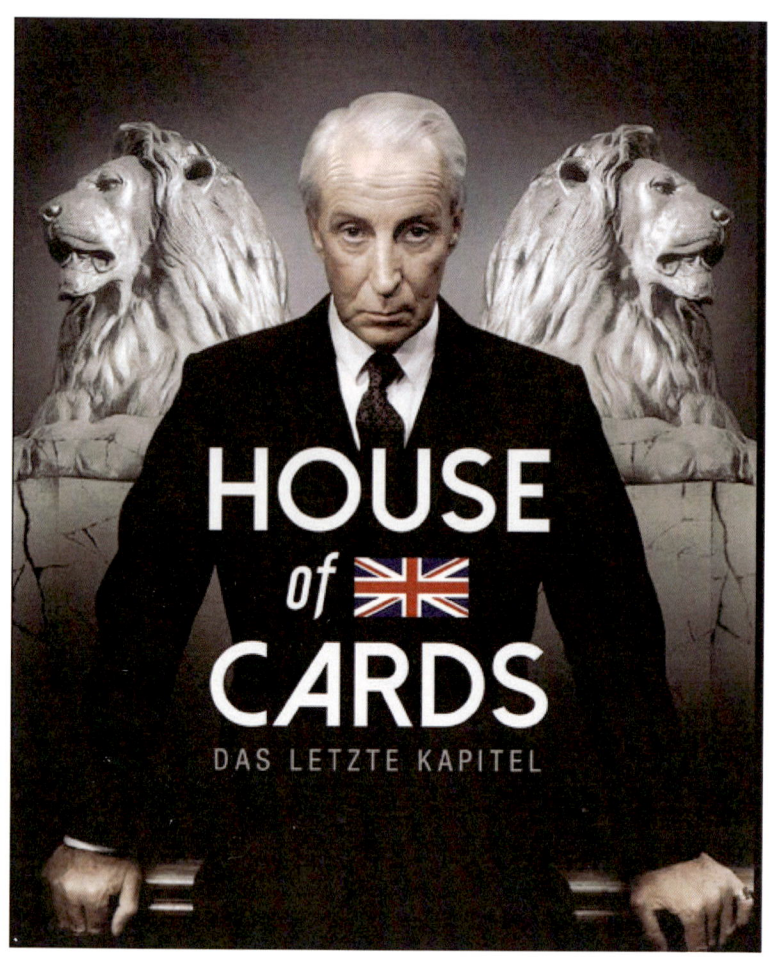

TV Poster

At home, Urquhart's wife says he is just the man to bring the downfall of the Prime Minister. She also encourages him to use Mattie Storin to help him along.

When the *Chronicle* prints a story criticizing the government-especially the Home Secretary and the prime Minister-an angry Collingridge calls Francis. "They're supposed to be our people!" Collingridge shouts. Urquhart says to leave things in his capable hands.

David Lyon as the P.M.

Nicholas Selby, Damien Thomas, Kenneth Gilbert, David Lyon, Malcolm Tierney, Christopher Owen, Ian Richardson

After blackmailing cocaine-addicted Roger O'Neill into being his informant, a number of questions come up in the House that prove embarrassing to the Prime Minister.

Meeting of the Cabinet

David Lyon, Kenneth Gilbert

Miles Anderson, Ian Richardson

Susannah Harker, Ian Richardson

Chaos erupts in the House when an opposition member brings up the hospital bill. Trying to answer the question, Collingridge is shouted down while the Speaker screams for order. Just what Urquhart wants.

Later, Urquhart sets up Charles Collingridge with the help of O'Neill and his girlfriend Penny Guy, as well as going to the bank himself in disguise and setting up phony accounts.

William Chubb, Susannah Harker, John Hartley

James Villiers, Susannah Harker

HOUSE OF CARDS EPISODE 2

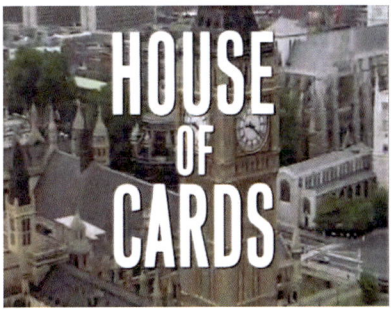

DIRECTED BY Paul Seed
ORIGINAL AIR DATE: 11/25/90

CAST

Ian Richardson.........Francis Urquhart
Susannah Harker............Mattie Storin
Miles Anderson............Roger O'Neill
David Lyon..P.M. Henry Collingridge
Malcolm Tierney.......Patrick Woolton
Nicholas Selby.......Lord Billsborough
Alphonsia Emmanuel........Penny Guy
James Villiers.....Charles Collingridge
Diane Fletcher......Elizabeth Urquhart
Kenny Ireland................Ben Landless
Isabelle Amyes........Ann Collingridge
William Chubb...........John Krajewski
John Hartley..............Greville Preston
Christopher Owen.....Peter McKenzie
Kenneth Gilbert..............Harold Earle
Colin Jeavons.................Tim Stamper
Damien Thomas......Michael Samuels
Peter Gale..............Political Secretary
John Arnatt...........Sir Jasper Grainger
Raymond Mason.........................Stoat
Geoffrey Bateman............Interviewer

Ian Richardson   Susannah Harker

Miles Anderson   David Lyon

Malcolm Tierney   Nicholas Selby

Alphonsia Emmanuel   James Villiers

Hugh Dickson...Dr. Andrew Christian
Richard Braine..............Kevin Spence
Justine Glenton......................P.R. Girl
Nick Brimble..........................Corder
Kevork Malikyan..............Mr. Naresh
Leslie Mills..........................Detective
Keturah Sorrell....Lady at Conference

Diane Fletcher   Kenny Ireland

AND: Mark Abbott, Joy Adams, Liz
Adams, Nancy Adams, Steve A'Dor,
Francis Agnew, Steve Aliffe, Jack

Isabelle Amyes   William Chubb

Armstrong, Yvonne Ash, Andrea Ashley, Richard Ashley, Robert Ashley-
Moore, Patricia Astley, Richard Atherton, David Bache, Norman Bacon, Jon

John Hartley   Christopher Owen

Baker, Samantha Baker, Colin Bald-
win, Gregory Ball, Rosemary Banks,
Anthony Barratt, Kip Barrs, Ilana
Barry, Tammy Bass, Francis Batsoni,

Kenneth Gilbert   Colin Jeavons

Samantha Beale, Paul Beaumont, Jason Beazley, Bernard Bennett, Alice
Benson, Barbara Bermel, Bobby Bernard, Peter Bex, David Billa, Hilary

Damien Thomas   Peter Gale

Bishop, Jane Bishop, Pete Blacker,
Nicholas Blatt, Karen Bourne, Peggy
Bourne, Andrew Bowen, Willy Bow-
man, Tommy Boyle, Mark Breckon,

Raymond Mason   Geoffrey Bateman

Mark Brett, Monique Briant, Michael
Britton-Jones, Oliver Broome, Mike
Brown, John Buckland, David Bul-
beck, Jack Burns, Stephen Calcutt,
Amanda Carlson, Fran Carder, Sandi
Carter, Con Chambers, Ray Chaney,
Jean Channon, Arnold Chazen, Johnny

Clamp, Ina Clare, Ann Clarke, Melita Clarke, Micky Clarke, Trisha Clarke, Helena Clayton, David Cleeve, Lindsey Cole, Michael Cole, Mair Coleman, Judy Collins, Ken Coombs, Eric Corlett, Judy Cowne, Ron Cozzi, Pamela Craine, Robert Crake, Chris Cresswell, Alan Crisp, Bert Crome, Jennifer Crome, Cyril Crook, Avril Dean, Jim Delany, Jan Denham, Terrance Denville, John Emms, Valerie Eve, Jill Fentiman, Keith Ferrari, Peter Finn, Simon Fisher-Becker, Carole Fisher-Grant, Noel Flanagan, Christian Fletcher, Alison Ford, Ruby Fox, Sally Fox, Irene Frederic, Jack Frost, Iris Fry, Ann Gabrielle, Paul Galloway, Salo Gardner, Martin Garfield, David Garry, Helen Garton, Alec Gifford, Selena Gilbert, Vivienne Glance, Alan Gold, Jill Goldston, Jenny Goodall, Laurie Goode, Vanessa Goodwright, Pat Gorman, Paul Govas, Alan Gray, Charlie Gray, Chrissie Grech, Christina Green, Ron Gregory, Jan Griffiths, Donald Groves, Dorothy Grumbar, Eldon Guller, Jean Hall, Mark Hallett, Adrian Hammond, June Hammond, Dave Hampson, Dick Harris, Gordon Harris, Paul Hart, John Hartley, Frank Harvey, Lloyd Harvey, Pearl Hawkes, Glen Hayes, Mandy Hearnden, Bill Hemmings, Carla Hendricks, Judy Herbert, Christine Hewitt, Vanessa

Hugh Dickson

Richard Braine

Girl

Man 1

Man 2

Man 3

Man 4

Reporter

Woman 1

Woman 2

Woman 3

Heywood, Kit Hillier, David Hillman, Josephine Hinchley, Freddie Hogarth, Barrie Holland, Ray Holland, Lew Hooper, Dick Hope, Clive Hopkins, Elaine Hopkins, Diane Horsey, Terri Howard, Paul Howlett, Ivor Humphris, Derek Hunt, Graham Hunter, John Huntley, Clive Hurst, Caroline Huxley, Cavid Ianson, Steve Ismay, Barbara Jaeson, Humph James, Juliette James, Lawrie James, Bernard Jamieson, Graham Jarvis, Kevin Jarvis, Ian Jason, Geraldine Jay, Simon Joseph, Paul Joy, Helen Judson, Luke Kelly, Rick Kennedy, Eric Kent, Leo Kersley, Richard King, Audrey Kirby, Mark Kirby, Paul Kirby, Harry Klein, Penny Lambirth, Ken Lawrie, Michael Leader, Pat LeClerc, Aileen Lewis, Alex Lewis, Debbie Lloyd, Peter Lloyd, Joan Lovelace, Ann Luksys, Maggie Lynton, Jay McGrath, Alison McGuire, Wyn McLeod, Ronald Markham, John Marley, Kay Marshall, Raymond Martin, Tina Maskell, Raymond Mason, Gary Matthews, Gina Maufe, Mary Maxted, Kate Meadows, David Melbourne, Ken Mercer, Julie Michelle, Ellen Miller, Nicolle Mills, Gareth Milne, Maggie Mitchell, Peter Moore, Julie Morgan, Brian Morgan-Carter, Jo Montgomery, John J. Moore, Lola Morice, James Muir, Mike Mulloy, Fiona Murray, Gary Murray, Honor Myers, Stuart Myers, Maureen Nelson, Jacqueline Noble, Lloyd Notice, Susan Nye, Kevin O'Brien, Tony O'Leary, Marie O'Mahoney, Gabrielle Parker, Tony Parkin, Oscar Peck, David Pelton, Pat Pelton, John Perrin, Patsy Peters, Joe Phillips, Noreen Phillips, Selwyn Pitcher, Bronek Pomorski, Adam Poulton, Brychan Powell, Sheila Power, Kaye Power-McGowan, Ken Pritchard, Paul Puig, Caroline Quennell, Susan Raasay, Celia Radband, Michael Reeves, Fred Reford, Leslie Rhodes, Lee Richards, Joseph Riordan, Evan Ross, David Rowley, Philip Sadler, Nicky Sands, Ivan Santon, John Sargent, Terry Sartain,

Eddy May Scandrett, Monty Scott, Roy Seeley, Grant Shelley, Pat Shepherd, Larry Sheppard, Roland Sidwell, Sally Sinclair, Harjit Singh, Virginia Slade, Barbara Smith, Edwina Smith, Robert Smythe, Anthony Snell, Judd Solo, Sharon St. Clare, Guy Standeven, Douglas Stark, Tony Starr, Sarah Jane Stedman, Lionel Stevens, Maureen Stevens, Marcus Still, David Stowell, Yvonne Stroud, Gary Sutcliffe, Derek Suthern, Keith Swaden, Paul Symington, Judy Szucs, Sue Tarry, Colin Thomas, Reg Thomason, Cy Town, Frank Tregear, Patricia Turton, Chris Underhill, Alan Uttley-Moore, Harry Van Engel, Derek Van Weenen, Janet Varley, Mike Vaughan, Annette Vellender, Christine Walker, Jay Watson, Jeff Wayne, Trevor Wedlock, Leslie Weekes, David Weller, Arthur Wells, Joe Wells, Joe Wenborne, Barbara Whateley, Lionel Wheeler, Eddie Whiting, Alan Wicks, Barrie Wilkinson, Elaine Williams, Llewellyn Williams, Raymond Williams, Trevor Willis, Sachaley Wilson, Stuart Windsor, Sue Winkler, Tony Winn, Tina Winter, Jana Winward, Tommy Winward, Kay Woodgate, Syd Wragg, Mavis Wright

The beleaguered prime minister and his colleagues have decamped to Brighton for the party conference. Urquhart acidly rates the performances of his colleagues, all of whom are subtly auditioning for the PM's job.

Francis Urqhart continues his surreptitious campaign to force Prime Minister Henry Collingridge's resignation. He says that he is a man who cannot bear to be idle. We need to keep Charles and Henry Collingwood in the public eye.

Susannah Harker, Ian Richardson

James Villiers, Susannah Harker

Ian Richardson, Kenny Ireland

Geoffrey Bateman as Interviewer

Through the Party's PR expert Roger O'Neill-who has had his fingers in the till and has also developed a cocaine habit-Urquhart arranges for opposition MPs to have access to Cabinet decisions making for an uncomfortable time in the House.

David Lyon, Susannah Harker

David Lyon et al

Urquhart blackmails O'Neill into delivering some secret and classified material to Mattie Storin, which O'Neill slips under her door anonymously in an envelope.

Ian Richardson, Susannah Harker

Miles Anderson, Alphonsia Emmanuel

Diane Fletcher, Ian Richardson

Susannah Harker, Ian Richardson

Through contacts with certain people, Mattie establishes the fact that the documents she was given are in fact genuine. Meanwhile, Urquhart continues to sow the seeds of mistrust within the government.

Finally, Urquhart lays the foundation for a money scandal. After having her story rejected by her bosses at The Chronicle, Mattie heads to a bar where she meets the P.M.s brother Charles.

Television Poster

Urquhart meets newspaper owner Ben Landless, who tells him that he quashed the story, That's not what Urquhart wanted. He says the P.M. is a weakling; rather than Collingridge, Patrick Woolton should lead the government.

Urquhart addresses the camera

Ian Richardson, Susannah Harker

TV Poster

Ian Richardson, Diane Fletcher

Ian Richardson as Francis Urquhart

Mattie is upset when she sees the story in the paper after she was told it was killed, and realizes the government is getting ready to junk Collingridge. Woolton says it's a bad business, but is secretly pleased.

Alphonsia Emmanuel, Miles Anderson

Ian Richardson, David Lyon

William Chubb, Susannah Harker

Raymond Mason, Ian Richardson

In a fit of pique and panic, Collingridge sacks Lord Billsborough, the party chairman, the greatly loved and longest serving member of the government, following a lacklustre speech by the P.M.

HOUSE OF CARDS EPISODE 3

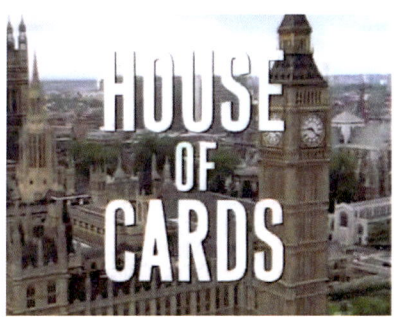

DIRECTED BY Paul Seed
ORIGINAL AIR DATE: 12/2/90

CAST

Ian Richardson.........Francis Urquhart
Susannah Harker............Mattie Storin
David Lyon.....P.M. Henry Collingridge
Miles Anderson............Roger O'Neill
Malcolm Tierney.......Patrick Woolton
Alphonsia Emmanuel........Penny Guy
James Villiers.....Charles Collingridge
Kenny Ireland................Ben Landless
Diane Fletcher......Elizabeth Urquhart
Isabelle Amyes........Ann Collingridge
Colin Jeavons.................Tim Stamper
Damien Thomas......Michael Samuels
Christopher Owen.....Peter McKenzie
Kenneth Gilbert..............Harold Earle
William Chubb...........John Krajewski
John Hartley..............Greville Preston
Richard Braine..............Kevin Spence
Hugh Dickson...Dr. Andrew Christian
Bill Wallis................Prestatyn Powell
Nick Brimble..........................Corder
Kevork Malikyan..............Mr. Naresh

Ian Richardson   Susannah Harker

David Lyon   Miles Anderson

Malcolm Tierney   Alphonsia Emmanuel

James Villiers   Kenny Ireland

Leslie Mills...........................Detective
Subash Singh Pall......................Waiter
Ian Collier.......................Man at Clinic
John Duval........................Young Man
Hattye Knight...............Black Woman
Lucy Christy, Angela Rippon..............
....Newsreaders

Diane Fletcher

Isabelle Amyes

AND: Mark Abbott, Joy Adams, Liz
Adams, Nancy Adams, Steve A'Dor,
Francis Agnew, Steve Aliffe, Jack
Armstrong, Yvonne Ash, Andrea Ash-
ley, Richard Ashley, Robert Ashley-
Moore, Patricia Astley, Richard Ather-
ton, David Bache, Norman Bacon, Jon
Baker, Samantha Baker, Colin Bald-
win, Gregory Ball, Rosemary Banks,
Anthony Barratt, Kip Barrs, Ilana
Barry, Tammy Bass, Francis Batsoni,
Samantha Beale, Paul Beaumont, Ja-
son Beazley, Bernard Bennett, Alice
Benson, Barbara Bermel, Bobby Ber-
nard, Peter Bex, David Billa, Hilary
Bishop, Jane Bishop, Pete Blacker,
Nicholas Blatt, Karen Bourne, Peggy
Bourne, Andrew Bowen, Willy Bow-
man, Tommy Boyle, Mark Breckon,
Mark Brett, Monique Briant, Michael
Britton-Jones, Oliver Broome, Mike
Brown, John Buckland, David Bul-
beck, Jack Burns, Stephen Calcutt,
Amanda Carlson, Fran Carder, Sandi
Carter, Con Chambers, Ray Chaney,
Jean Channon, Arnold Chazen, John-

Colin Jeavons

Damien Thomas

Christopher Owen

Kenneth Gilbert

William Chubb

John Hartley

Richard Braine

Hugh Dickson

Bill Wallis

Ian Collier

ny Clamp, Ina Clare, Ann Clarke, Melita Clarke, Micky Clarke, Trisha Clarke, Helena Clayton, David Cleeve, Lindsey Cole, Michael Cole, Mair Coleman, Judy Collins, Ken Coombs, Eric Corlett, Judy Cowne, Ron Cozzi, Pamela Craine, Robert Crake, Chris Cresswell, Alan Crisp, Bert Crome, Jennifer Crome, Cyril Crook, Avril Dean, Jim Delany, Jan Denham, Terrance Denville, John Emms, Valerie Eve, Jill Fentiman, Keith Ferrari, Peter Finn, Simon Fisher-Becker, Carole Fisher-Grant, Noel Flanagan, Christian Fletcher, Alison Ford, Ruby Fox, Sally Fox, Irene Frederic, Jack Frost, Iris Fry, Ann Gabrielle, Paul Galloway, Salo Gardner, Martin Garfield, David Garry, Helen Garton, Alec Gifford, Selena Gilbert, Vivienne Glance, Alan Gold, Jill Goldston, Jenny Goodall, Laurie Goode, Vanessa Goodwright, Pat Gorman, Paul Govas, Alan Gray, Charlie Gray, Chrissie Grech, Christina Green, Ron Gregory, Jan Griffiths,

Angela Rippon   Ken Coombs

Cabinet Minister 1   Cabinet Minister 2

Cabinet Minister 3   Man

Woman 1   Woman 1

Donald Groves, Dorothy Grumbar, Eldon Guller, Jean Hall, Mark Hallett, Adrian Hammond, June Hammond, Dave Hampson, Dick Harris, Gordon Harris, Paul Hart, John Hartley, Frank Harvey, Lloyd Harvey, Pearl Hawkes, Glen Hayes, Mandy Hearnden, Bill Hemmings, Carla Hendricks, Judy Herbert, Christine Hewitt, Van

43

essa Heywood, Kit Hillier, David Hillman, Josephine Hinchley, Freddie Hogarth, Barrie Holland, Ray Holland, Lew Hooper, Dick Hope, Clive Hopkins, Elaine Hopkins, Diane Horsey, Terri Howard, Paul Howlett, Ivor Humphris, Derek Hunt, Graham Hunter, John Huntley, Clive Hurst, Caroline Huxley, Cavid Ianson, Steve Ismay, Barbara Jaeson, Humph James, Juliette James, Lawrie James, Bernard Jamieson, Graham Jarvis, Kevin Jarvis, Ian Jason, Geraldine Jay, Simon Joseph, Paul Joy, Helen Judson, Luke Kelly, Rick Kennedy, Eric Kent, Leo Kersley, Richard King, Audrey Kirby, Mark Kirby, Paul Kirby, Harry Klein, Penny Lambirth, Ken Lawrie, Michael Leader, Pat LeClerc, Aileen Lewis, Alex Lewis, Debbie Lloyd, Peter Lloyd, Joan Lovelace, Ann Luksys, Maggie Lynton, Jay McGrath, Alison McGuire, Wyn McLeod, Ronald Markham, John Marley, Kay Marshall, Raymond Martin, Tina Maskell, Raymond Mason, Gary Matthews, Gina Maufe, Mary Maxted, Kate Meadows, David Melbourne, Ken Mercer, Julie Michelle, Ellen Miller, Nicolle Mills, Gareth Milne, Maggie Mitchell, Peter Moore, Julie Morgan, Brian Morgan-Carter, Jo Montgomery, John J. Moore, Lola Morice, James Muir, Mike Mulloy, Fiona Murray, Gary Murray, Honor Myers, Stuart Myers, Maureen Nelson, Jacqueline Noble, Lloyd Notice, Susan Nye, Kevin O'Brien, Tony O'Leary, Marie O'Mahoney, Gabrielle Parker, Tony Parkin, Oscar Peck, David Pelton, Pat Pelton, John Perrin, Patsy Peters, Joe Phillips, Noreen Phillips, Selwyn Pitcher, Bronek Pomorski, Adam Poulton, Brychan Powell, Sheila Power, Kaye Power-McGowan, Ken Pritchard, Paul Puig, Caroline Quennell, Susan Raasay, Celia Radband, Michael Reeves, Fred Reford, Leslie Rhodes, Lee Richards, Joseph Riordan, Evan Ross, David Rowley, Philip Sadler, Nicky Sands, Ivan Santon, John Sargent, Terry Sartain,

Eddy May Scandrett, Monty Scott, Roy Seeley, Grant Shelley, Pat Shepherd, Larry Sheppard, Roland Sidwell, Sally Sinclair, Harjit Singh, Virginia Slade, Barbara Smith, Edwina Smith, Robert Smythe, Anthony Snell, Judd Solo, Sharon St. Clare, Guy Standeven, Douglas Stark, Tony Starr, Sarah Jane Stedman, Lionel Stevens, Maureen Stevens, Marcus Still, David Stowell, Yvonne Stroud, Gary Sutcliffe, Derek Suthern, Keith Swaden, Paul Symington, Judy Szucs, Sue Tarry, Colin Thomas, Reg Thomason, Cy Town, Frank Tregear, Patricia Turton, Chris Underhill, Alan Uttley-Moore, Harry Van Engel, Derek Van Weenen, Janet Varley, Mike Vaughan, Annette Vellender, Christine Walker, Jay Watson, Jeff Wayne, Trevor Wedlock, Leslie Weekes, David Weller, Arthur Wells, Joe Wells, Joe Wenborne, Barbara Whateley, Lionel Wheeler, Eddie Whiting, Alan Wicks, Barrie Wilkinson, Elaine Williams, Llewellyn Williams, Raymond Williams, Trevor Willis, Sachaley Wilson, Stuart Windsor, Sue Winkler, Tony Winn, Tina Winter, Jana Winward, Tommy Winward, Kay Woodgate, Syd Wragg, Mavis Wright

As scandals and leaked stories gain momentum, Collingridge finds himself in deep political trouble, and he has no alternative but to step down as Prime Minister.

The only man whom he feels he can still trust is Urquhart. The Prime Minister resigns and the race is on to replace him. Environment Minister Michael Samuels and Foreign Minister Patrick Woolton are the apparent front-runners, though the Chronicle newspaper comes out publicly in support of Urquhart.

Outside 10 Downing Street

Susannah Harker as Mattie Storin

David Lyon, James Villiers

Ian Richardson as Francis Urquhart

Urquhart once again addresses the viewing audience. "Not feeling guilty, I hope. If you have pangs of pity, crush them now. Grind them under your heel like old cigar butts.

Isabelle Amyes, Hugh Dickson

Susannah Harker, Ian Richardson

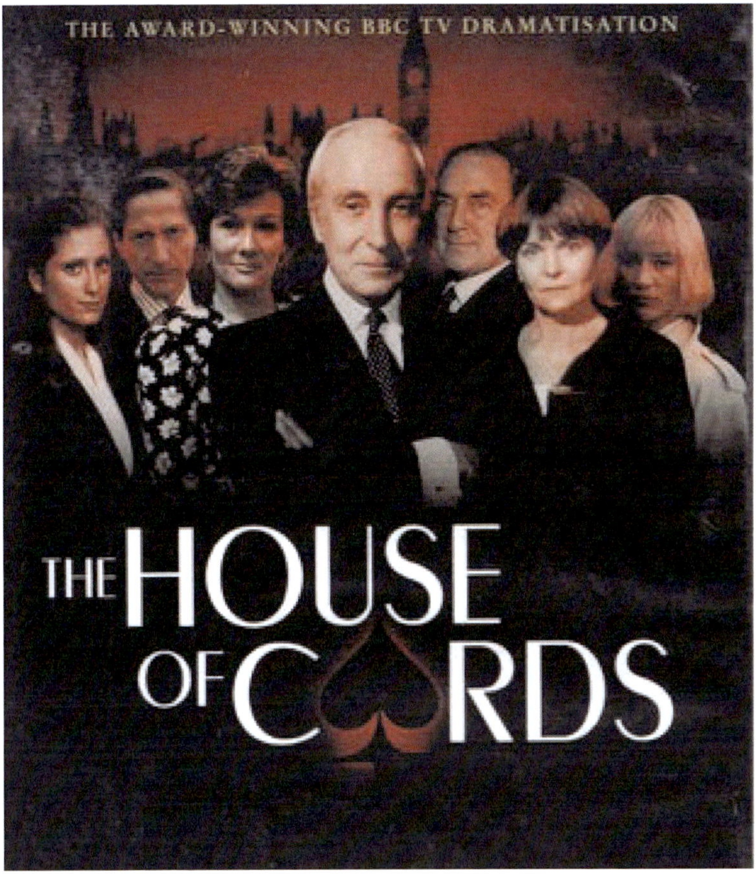

THE AWARD-WINNING BBC TV DRAMATISATION

THE HOUSE OF CARDS

TV Poster

Susannah Harker, James Villiers

TV Poster

I've done the country a favour. He didn't have the brain or the heart or the stomach to rule a country like Great Britain. A nice enough man, but there was no bottom to him. His deepest need was that people should like him. An admirable trait, that. In a spaniel or a whore. Not, I think in a Prime Minster."

At his wife's encouragement, Urquhart seduces journalist Mattie Storin but doesn't realize she recorded their conversation. She traces Charles Collingridge to the rehab center and begins to doubt that he was the engineer of the scandal.

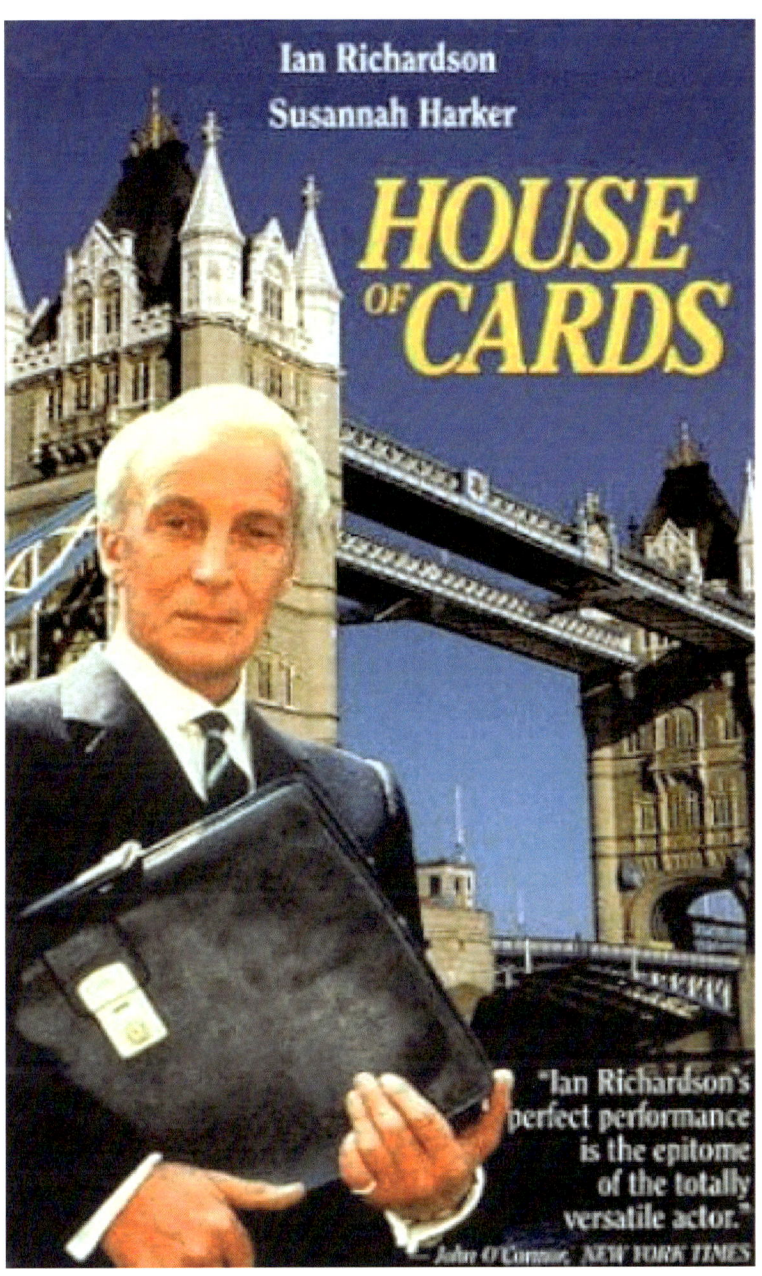

TV Poster

When she learns that someone altered the files at the Conservative central office, she has proof but her editor has different plans. When Urquhart learns that she's found Charles, he arranges for a clear message to be sent to her.

Kenny Ireland, Ian Richardson

David Lyon, James Villiers

Ian Richardson as Francis Urquhart

Ian Richardson, Susannah Harker

It seems clear that Henry Collingridge couldn't have bought the shares, since Charles convinces her that he's not got a great deal in the old brain.

John Krajewski warns Mattie that she is playing with dynamite-whoever was involved in the frame up knows she found Charles at the clinic, and also knows she is responsible for the story.

Diane Fletcher, Ian Richardson

Ken Coombs, Malcolm Tierney

Kenneth Gilbert, Damien Thomas

Ian Richardson with the cabinet

When Mattie phones Roger O'Neill, it's Penny Guy who meets with her instead. She says Roger was ordered to threaten her, but she does not know who was pulling the strings.

So can Francis Urquhart count on Mattie's loyalty? At present it seems so, but he isn't aware that she's been secretly tape-recording all of their meetings.

Another Cabinet scene

Susannah Harker, William Chubb

HOUSE OF CARDS EPISODE 4

DIRECTED BY Paul Seed
ORIGINAL AIR DATE: 12/9/90

CAST

Ian Richardson.........Francis Urquhart
Susannah Harker............Mattie Storin
Miles Anderson............Roger O'Neill
Diane Fletcher......Elizabeth Urquhart
Malcolm Tierney.......Patrick Woolton
Alphonsia Emmanuel........Penny Guy
Damien Thomas......Michael Samuels
Colin Jeavons.................Tim Stamper
Christopher Owen.....Peter McKenzie
Kenneth Gilbert..............Harold Earle
William Chubb...........John Krajewski
Robin Wentworth...Sir Humphrey Newlands
Vivienne Ritchie...Stephanie Woolton
Kevork Malikyan..............Mr. Naresh
Leslie Mills..........................Detective
Tommy Boyle.........Stephen Kendrick
Eric Allan.................Adrian Shepherd
Jan Winters.......McKenzie's Assistant
Kenneth Hadley....................Chauffer

Ian Richardson   Susannah Harker

Miles Anderson   Diane Fletcher

Malcolm Tierney   Alphonsia Emmanuel

Damien Thomas   Colin Jeavons

AND: Mark Abbott, Joy Adams, Liz Adams, Nancy Adams, Steve A'Dor, Francis Agnew, Steve Aliffe, Jack Armstrong, Yvonne Ash, Andrea Ashley, Richard Ashley, Robert Ashley-Moore, Patricia Astley, Richard Atherton, David Bache, Norman Bacon, Jon Baker, Samantha Baker, Colin Baldwin, Gregory Ball, Rosemary Banks, Anthony Barratt, Kip Barrs, Ilana Barry, Tammy Bass, Francis Batsoni, Samantha Beale, Paul Beaumont, Jason Beazley, Bernard Bennett, Alice Benson, Barbara Bermel, Bobby Bernard, Peter Bex, David Billa, Hilary Bishop, Jane Bishop, Pete Blacker, Nicholas Blatt, Karen Bourne, Peggy Bourne, Andrew Bowen, Willy Bowman, Tommy Boyle, Mark Breckon, Mark Brett, Monique Briant, Michael Britton-Jones, Oliver Broome, Mike Brown, John Buckland, David Bulbeck, Jack Burns, Stephen Calcutt, Amanda Carlson, Fran Carder, Sandi Carter, Con Chambers, Ray Chaney, Jean Channon, Arnold Chazen, Johnny Clamp, Ina Clare, Ann Clarke, Melita Clarke, Micky Clarke, Trisha Clarke, Helena Clayton, David Cleeve, Lindsey Cole, Michael Cole, Mair Coleman, Judy Collins, Ken Coombs, Eric Corlett, Judy Cowne, Ron Cozzi, Pamela Craine, Robert Crake, Chris Cresswell, Alan Crisp, Bert Crome,

Christopher Owen

Kenneth Gilbert

William Chubb

Robin Wentworth

Vivienne Ritchie

Tommy Boyle

Eric Allan

Jan Winters

Syd Wragg

Reporter 1

Reporter 2

Jennifer Crome, Cyril Crook, Avril Dean, Jim Delany, Jan Denham, Terrance Denville, John Emms, Valerie Eve, Jill Fentiman, Keith Ferrari, Peter Finn, Simon Fisher-Becker, Carole Fisher-Grant, Noel Flanagan, Christian Fletcher, Alison Ford, Ruby Fox, Sally Fox, Irene Frederic, Jack Frost, Iris Fry, Ann Gabrielle, Paul Galloway, Salo Gardner, Martin Garfield, David Garry, Helen Garton, Alec Gifford, Selena Gilbert, Vivienne Glance, Alan Gold, Jill Goldston, Jenny Goodall, Laurie Goode, Vanessa Goodwright, Pat Gorman, Paul Govas, Alan Gray, Charlie Gray, Chrissie Grech, Christina Green, Ron Gregory, Jan Griffiths, Donald Groves, Dorothy Grumbar, Eldon Guller, Jean Hall, Mark Hallett, Adrian Hammond, June Hammond, Dave Hampson, Dick Harris, Gordon Harris, Paul Hart, John Hartley, Frank Harvey, Lloyd Harvey, Pearl Hawkes, Glen Hayes, Mandy Hearnden, Bill Hemmings, Carla Hendricks, Judy Herbert, Christine Hewitt, Vanessa Heywood, Kit Hillier, David Hillman, Josephine Hinchley, Freddie Hogarth, Barrie Holland, Ray Holland, Lew Hooper, Dick Hope, Clive Hopkins, Elaine Hopkins, Diane Horsey, Terri Howard, Paul Howlett, Ivor Humphris, Derek Hunt, Graham Hunter, John Huntley, Clive Hurst, Caroline Huxley, Cavid Ianson, Steve Ismay, Barbara Jaeson, Humph James, Juliette James, Lawrie James, Bernard Jamieson, Graham Jarvis, Kevin Jarvis, Ian Jason, Geraldine Jay, Simon Joseph, Paul Joy, Helen Judson, Luke Kelly, Rick Kennedy, Eric Kent, Leo Kersley, Richard King, Audrey Kirby, Mark Kirby, Paul Kirby, Harry Klein, Penny Lambirth, Ken Lawrie, Michael Leader, Pat LeClerc, Aileen Lewis, Alex Lewis, Debbie Lloyd, Peter Lloyd, Joan Lovelace, Ann Luksys, Maggie Lynton, Jay McGrath, Alison McGuire, Wyn McLeod, Ronald Markham, John Marley, Kay Marshall, Raymond Martin, Tina Maskell, Raymond Mason, Gary Matthews, Gina Maufe, Mary Maxted, Kate Meadows, David Melbourne, Ken Mercer, Julie Michelle, Ellen Miller, Nicolle Mills, Gareth Milne, Maggie Mitchell, Peter Moore, Julie Morgan, Brian Morgan-Carter, Jo Montgomery, John J. Moore, Lola Morice, James Muir, Mike Mulloy, Fiona Murray, Gary Murray, Honor Myers, Stuart Myers, Maureen Nelson, Jacqueline Noble, Lloyd Notice, Susan Nye, Kevin O'Brien, Tony O'Leary, Marie O'Mahoney, Gabrielle Parker, Tony Parkin, Oscar Peck, David Pelton, Pat Pelton, John Perrin, Patsy Peters, Joe Phillips, Noreen Phillips, Selwyn Pitcher, Bronek Pomorski, Adam Poulton, Brychan Powell, Sheila Power, Kaye Power-McGowan, Ken Pritchard, Paul Puig, Caroline Quennell, Susan Raasay, Celia Radband, Michael Reeves, Fred Reford, Leslie Rhodes, Lee Richards, Joseph Riordan, Evan Ross, David Rowley, Philip Sadler, Nicky Sands, Ivan Santon, John Sargent, Terry Sartain, Eddy May Scandrett, Monty Scott, Roy Seeley, Grant Shelley, Pat Shepherd, Larry Sheppard, Roland Sidwell, Sally Sinclair, Harjit Singh, Virginia Slade, Barbara Smith, Edwina Smith, Robert Smythe, Anthony Snell, Judd Solo, Sharon St. Clare, Guy Standeven, Douglas Stark, Tony Starr, Sarah Jane Stedman, Lionel Stevens, Maureen Stevens, Marcus Still, David Stowell, Yvonne Stroud, Gary Sutcliffe, Derek Suthern, Keith Swaden, Paul Symington, Judy Szucs, Sue Tarry, Colin Thomas, Reg Thomason, Cy Town, Frank Tregear, Patricia Turton, Chris Underhill, Alan Uttley-Moore, Harry Van Engel, Derek Van Weenen, Janet Varley, Mike Vaughan, Annette Vellender, Christine Walker, Jay Watson, Jeff Wayne, Trevor Wedlock, Leslie Weekes, David Weller, Arthur Wells, Joe Wells, Joe Wenborne, Barbara Whateley, Lionel Wheeler, Eddie Whiting, Alan Wicks, Barrie Wilkinson, Elaine Williams, Llewellyn Williams,

Raymond Williams, Trevor Willis, Sachaley Wilson, Stuart Windsor, Sue Winkler, Tony Winn, Tina Winter, Jana Winward, Tommy Winward, Kay Woodgate, Syd Wragg, Mavis Wright

Urquhart announces his intention to seek the leadership of the Conservative Party and become Prime Minister. Urquhart's ruthless scheming is working.

Ian Richardson, Colin Jeavons

As the leadership election looms, all his leading rivals have been discredited. But even though the obstacles in his way have been erased, there is still no guarantee of his winning.

Ian Richardson as Francis Urquhart

William Chubb, Susannah Harker

Ian Richardson as Francis Urquhart

The end of Mattie

It's six days until the first ballot and Urquhart plots against his rivals. One by one, the minor candidates fall by the wayside. Meanwhile, the truth is beginning to dawn on Mattie. As for Urquhart, he has too much to lose to let sentiment stand in his way.

Health minister Michael Samuels has an accident. Patrick Woolton gets tripped up by the recording of him in bed at the party conference and throws his support to Francis.

Location Scene

Ian Richardson, Miles Anderson

Ian Richardson, Colin Jeavons

Vivienne Ritchie, Malcolm Tierney

Next up is Harold Earle. He was tangled up with a rent-boy on a train some years ago, although it was all hushed up. Urquhart wryly observes that it would be very bad form to bring it all up again.

Map with marked location

Confrontation on the roof

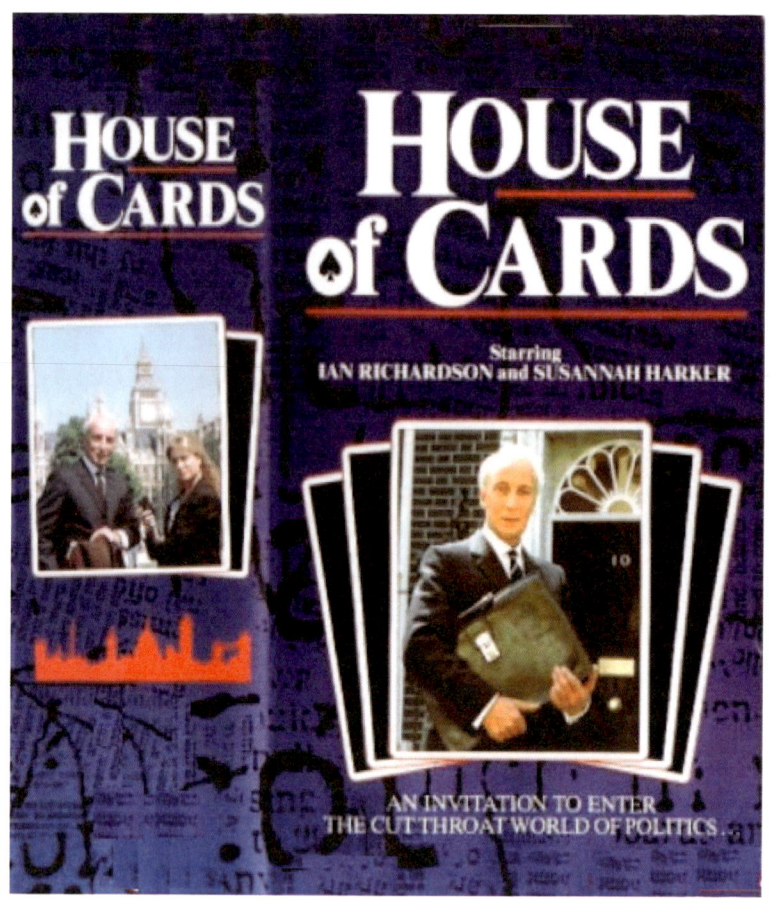

TV Poster

Stamper counters that "getting sucked off for six-pence in a second class compartment is hardly prime ministerial behaviour." A few pictures sent to Earle is enough to convince him that he should step down from the race.

Patrick Woolton later tells his wife the reason why he decided to support Urquhart – and it wasn't out of friendship. He believes that Samuels and Lord Billsborough engineered his downfall, so whilst he may dislike Urquhart he detests Samuels.

Location scene

Malcolm Tierney looks uncomfortable

Another small detail is when he tells her that it's also worth supporting Urquhart because he's the older man. Old men die sooner and the sooner Urquhart dies, the quicker Patrick Woolton will be back.

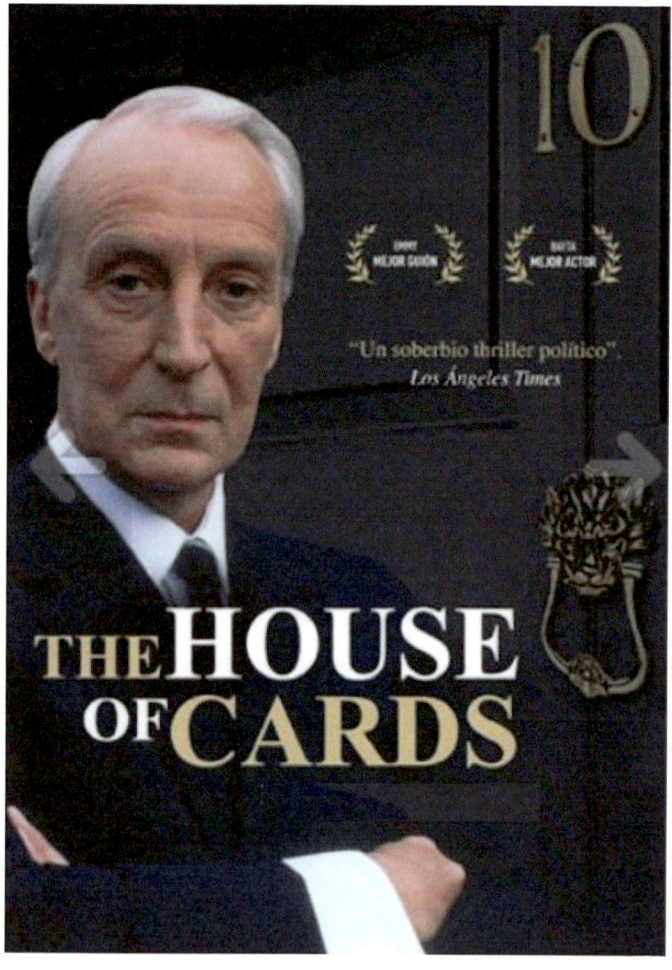

TV Poster

Mattie flies off the roof

With the house of cards beginning to wobble, Urquhart has to go to even greater lengths to protect himself. Roger O'Neill is clearly a liability, so Urquhart
invites him down to his country house, gets him
drunk and then laces his cocaine with rat poison.

Francis looks at the camera and says "This is an act of mercy. Truly. You know the man now. You can see he has nowhere to go. He's begging to be set free. He's had enough. And when he's finally at rest, then we'll be free to remember the real Roger."

Ian Richardson on the phone

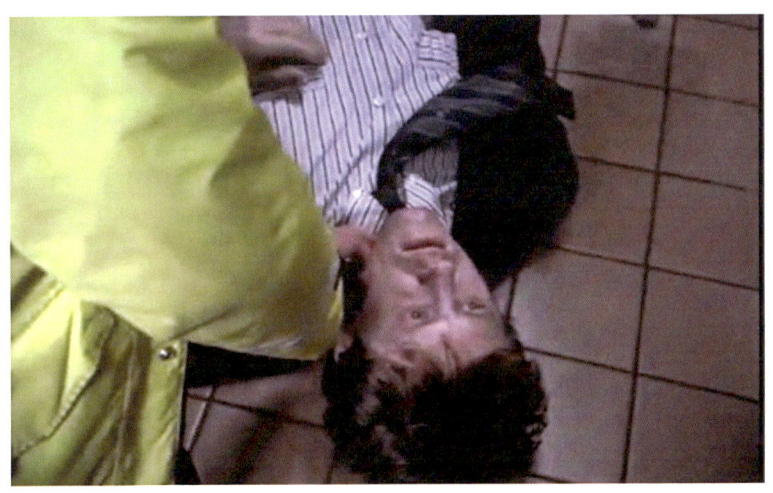

Miles Anderson, deceased

Susannah Harker, William Chubb

Thanks to a replay of Mattie's various audio tapes, she begins to piece everything together; she finds Urquhart at the House of Commons roof garden where things come to a head.

When she confronts him, he suddenly grabs her and throws her off the roof to her death. "I had to do it-how could I have trusted her?" he says. "You might very well think that. I could not possibly comment."

Susannah Harker as Mattie Storin

TO PLAY THE KING EPISODE 1

DIRECTED BY Paul Seed
ORIGINAL AIR DATE: 11/21/93

CAST

Ian Richardson.........Francis Urquhart
Michael Kitchen.........................King
Kitty Aldridge..............Sarah Harding
Colin Jeavons.................Tim Stamper
Nicholas Farrell...........David Mycroft
Diane Fletcher......Elizabeth Urquhart
Leonard Preston...............John Stroud
Rowena King.........Chloe Carmichael
Frederick Treves......Lord Quillington
David Ryall...........Sir Bruce Bullerby
Pip Torrens...............Andrew Harding
Michael Howarth..............Dick Caule
Merelina Kendall...Hilda Cordwainer
Barry Linehan...............Henry Hotson
Nick Brimble...........................Corder
Bernice Stegers......Princess Charlotte
Jack Fortune...........Ken Charterhouse
Erika Hoffman.....................The Lady
Tom Beasley..................Young Prince
Don Warrington...........Graham Gaunt
Terry Woodfield......................Barman

Ian Richardson

Michael Kitchen

Kitty Aldridge

Colin Jeavons

Nicholas Farrell

Diane Fletcher

Leonard Preston

Rowena King

Paula Tilbrook.........................Speaker
Joanna Archer-Nicholls.....Young Girl
Ryan Hurst...........................Page Boy
Susannah Harker............Mattie Storin
Sonya Kearns, Alex Walkinshaw........
....Muggers

Frederick Treves

David Ryall

Pip Torrens

Michael Howarth

Merelina Kendall

Barry Linehan

Nick Brimble

Bernice Stegers

Jack Fortune

Erika Hoffman

Tom Beasley

Don Warrington

AND: Michael Ackerman, David Adams, Kitty Aldridge, Dane Alexander, Mark Allington, Lee Alliston, Miles Ambrose, David Arnold, Richard Ashley, Jackie Avey, Fiona Baker, Micky Baker, Rosemary Banks, Jackie Barnes, Andy Barrett, Julian Barsham, Adrian Bell, Andrew Bell, Simon Bell, Adrian Bennett, Gary Bentley, June Bernice, David Billa, Ezra Bix, Judith Blakstad, George Blee, Jane Bough, Willy Bowman, Ray Boyd, Mark Brett, Annie Bright, Mervyn Brooker, Ingrid Bradley, James Bulbeck, Tina Bunnag, Nick Burgess, Sophie Burnham, Patricia Butler, Roy Byrne, Woolf Byrne, Yvonne Byrne, Graham Carrigan, Guy Carter, Graham Case, Con Chambers, Elizabeth Chambers, Jean Channon, Mark Chapman, William Chubb, Melita Clarke, Trisha Clarke, Helena Clayton, John Clements, Michael Cole, Mair Coleman, Judy Collins, Keith Connolly, Peter Cooney, June Cooper, Malcolm Cooper, Judy Cowne,

Pamela Craine, Derek Currell, Paul Dark, John Darling, Cyril Davey, Tom Deluvian, Terrance Denville, Serena Destouche, John Dodd, Chris Dyson, Ian Easton, Jon Fedyk, Sybil Ferguson, Keith Ferrari, Joan Field, Jeremy Fine, Peter Finn, Stephen Fitzalan, Christian Fletcher, Ray Flight, Patrick Ford, Gary Forecast, Terry Forrestal, Sally Fox, Robert Frank, Kathleen Fraser, Iris Fry, Ricky Galahad, Paul Galloway, Caron Gardner, Martin Garfield, Jo Gibson, Alec Gifford, Kenneth Gilbert, Donald Gilbey, Ann Gilliam, George Gilmour, Alan Gold, Laurie Goode, Carole Anne Goodman, Pat Gorman, Paul Govas, Lynn Gray, Anita Green, Jan Griffiths, Elizabeth Gronow, Trevor St. John Hacker, Adrian Hammond, Dave Hampson, Mike Harris, Paul Harris, Jean Hastings, Cassie Hatton, Glen Hayes, Ken Hazeldine, Aaron Heard, Gabrielle Hecht, Nick Helder, Judy Herbert, Andy Herrity, Tom Hibbert, George Higgins,

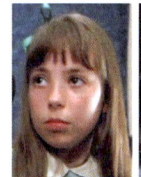 

Joanna Archer-Nicholls   Susannah Harker

Alex Walkinshaw   Butler

Cabinet Member   Foreign Dignitary

Pub Patron

Kit Hillier, Lew Hooper, Dick Hope, Clive Hopkins, Vivianne Horne, Clive Hurst, Philip Ingham, Paul Irving, Harry Isaacs, Jason Ives, Juliette James, Tex James, Charles Jiminez, Joanne Johnstone, Barrie Jones, Cori Josias, Simon Kane, Michael Kaufman, Rick Kennedy, Mike Kent, Paul Kirby, Harry Klein, Francesca Lacey, Penny Lambirth, Barbara Lampshire, Terra Landers, Paul Langley, Lisa Law, Ken Lawrie, Pat LeClerc, Irene Leigh, Debbie Lloyd, Roger Low, Don McLean, Della McRae, Ben Mansworth, Paul Markham, Ronald Markham, John Marley, Raymond Martin, Tina Maskell, Stephen Mason, Ken Mercer, Lawrence Merry, Nicola Miles, Ellen Miller, George Miller, Richard Moody, Brian Moorehead, Brian Morgan-Carter, Dermot Mulqueen, Mike Mungarvan, Jonathan Murray, Stuart Myers, Nilar Myin, Frank Neary, Clive Norman, Cliffe Obaseki, Kevin O'Brien, Rowland Ogden, Mick Oliver, Mark O'Reilly, Lisa Page, Gabrielle Parker, Alisdair Paul, Sarah Perkins, Ray Pollington, Theo Pouros, Brychan Powell, Huw Prall, Ken Pritchard, Paul Puig, Susan Raasay, Prudence Rennick, Steve Rickard, Kevin Ryan, Simon Sands, Roy Seeley, John Sergeant, Carol Shaw, Larry Sheppard, Julian Sherman, Sally Sinclair, Graham Skidmore, Anthony Smee, Barbara Smith, Anthony Snell, Guy Standeven, Douglas Stark, Sarah-Jane Stedman, David Steele, Bernice Stegers, Graham Stevens, Kerry Stokes, Barry Summerford, Al Szucs, Dean Taylor, Kim Taylor, Andy Thompson, Clive Thompson, Mal Tobias, Cy Town, Frank Tregear, Felicity Trew, Kathryn Turner, Roger Turner, Marcus Tylor, Chris Underhill, Alan Uttley-Moore, Derek Van Weenen, Paul Vincent, Tricia Vincent, Sheila Vivien, Kelvin Warren, Jeff Wayne, Paul Weakley, Maxine Weavers, Kate Webb, Leslie Weekes, Joe Wells, Joe Wenborne, June West, Ken Whitfield, Alan Wicks, Danny Wilder, Renee Williams, Tony Winn, Tina Winter, Tommy Winward, Andrew Woodman, Arnold Zarom

Frances Urquhart is now Prime Minister and is somewhat haunted by what he has done in the past. A newly crowned King presents him with more of a challenge that he may have expected.

Ian Richardson, Kitty Aldridge

Ian Richardson, Michael Howarth

TV Poster

Urquhart at the breakfast table

Kitty Aldridge as Sarah Harding

Nicholas Farrell accosted

At their first meeting, the King calls Urquhart a clever man; the Prime Minister says he would rather be remembered as a wise man. The King wants to be remembered as a "good man," which he thinks may sound absurd.

The King has a conscience and to Urquhart's distress, wants to make a contribution. Urquhart doesn't stand by idly and the King's interest in a major urban renewal project means curtains for the Environment Secretary who proposed it.

Diane Fletcher, Nick Brimble, Ian Richardson

Ian Richardson, Michael Kitchen

Kitty Aldridge, Ian Richardson

Guests at the party

Meanwhile, the PM hires a new political adviser, Sarah Harding, and his right-hand man, Tim Stamper, puts into motion an insurance policy of sorts they've developed by co-opting a member of the Royal family, Princess Charlotte.

Diane Fletcher, Ian Richardson

The Urquharts at the coronation

Ian Richardson as Francis Urquhart

Michael Kitchen as the King

The King's refusal to change a speech where he is seemingly at odds with the government sets the wheels of his destruction in motion. Urquhart warns the King that in a constitutional monarch, the sovereign cannot be seen to publicly oppose his own government.

Urquhart calls on Sarah Harding to modify the speech, taking out all the "interesting bits," and substitute something warm and dry instead. She agrees with Urquhart, and will get it ready soon.

Frederick Treves, Bernice Stegers, David Ryall

Nicholas Farrell, Rowena King, Ian Richardson

Nicholas Farrell, Rowena King

The King is crowned

While this is going on, David Mycroft is attacked and robbed after having a few drinks in a pub. When he picks himself up, he meets man who buys him a drink-then takes Mycroft home with him. Uh-oh!

Urquhart goes to see the King, reading him the riot act. He says the leak about the attempted speech modification came from the palace, and he intends to find out how it originated.

Royal coach proceeds

Merelina Kendall, Colin Jeavons

TO PLAY THE KING EPISODE 2

DIRECTED BY Paul Seed
ORIGINAL AIR DATE: 11/28/93

CAST

Ian Richardson.........Francis Urquhart
Michael Kitchen..........................King
Kitty Aldridge...............Sarah Harding
Colin Jeavons.................Tim Stamper
Diane Fletcher......Elizabeth Urquhart
Rowena King.........Chloe Carmichael
Nicholas Farrell...........David Mycroft
Jack Fortune...........Ken Charterhouse
Bernice Stegers......Princess Charlotte
David Ryall...........Sir Bruce Bullerby
John Bird..........Brian Brynford-Jones
Frederick Treves......Lord Quillington
Pip Torrens...............Andrew Harding
Leonard Preston...............John Stroud
David Neville.................Salmon Pink
George Raistrick................Gropeham
Nick Brimble...........................Corder
Kenneth Gilbert..............Harold Earle
Christopher Owen..............McKenzie
Elizabeth Chambers.......Baroness Craske
Kate Ricketts.....Current Affairs Lady

Ian Richardson   Michael Kitchen

Kitty Aldridge   Colin Jeavons

Diane Fletcher   Rowena King

Nicholas Farrell   Jack Fortune

Erika Hoffman.....................The Lady
Emma Bunton......................Prostitute
Lucy Parker..........................Waitress
Peter Terry...........................Detective
Paula Terry..............................Speaker
Anthony Smee................John Staines
John Paul Connolly......Sturdy Beggar
Soo Drouet.......................Big Woman
Ryan Hurst...........................Page Boy
Susannah Harker............Mattie Storin

Bernice Stegers

David Ryall

John Bird

Frederick Treves

AND: Michael Ackerman, David
Adams, Kitty Aldridge, Dane Alex-
ander, Mark Allington, Lee Alliston,
Miles Ambrose, David Arnold, Rich-
ard Ashley, Jackie Avey, Fiona Baker,
Micky Baker, Rosemary Banks, Jackie
Barnes, Andy Barrett, Julian Barsham,
Adrian Bell, Andrew Bell, Simon Bell,
Adrian Bennett, Gary Bentley, June
Bernice, David Billa, Ezra Bix, Judith
Blakstad, George Blee, Jane Bough,
Willy Bowman, Ray Boyd, Mark
Brett, Annie Bright, Mervyn Brook-
er, Ingrid Bradley, James Bulbeck,
Tina Bunnag, Nick Burgess, Sophie
Burnham, Patricia Butler, Roy Byrne,
Woolf Byrne, Yvonne Byrne, Graham
Carrigan, Guy Carter, Graham Case,
Con Chambers, Elizabeth Chambers,
Jean Channon, Mark Chapman, Wil-
liam Chubb, Melita Clarke, Trisha
Clarke, Helena Clayton, John Cle-

Pip Torrens

Leonard Preston

David Neville

George Raistrick

Nick Brimble

Kenneth Gilbert

Christopher Owen

Elizabeth Chambers

ments, Michael Cole, Mair Coleman, Judy Collins, Keith Connolly, Peter Cooney, June Cooper, Malcolm Cooper, Judy Cowne, Pamela Craine, Derek Currell, Paul Dark, John Darling, Cyril Davey, Tom Deluvian, Terrance Denville, Serena Destouche, John Dodd, Chris Dyson, Ian Easton, Jon Fedyk, Sybil Ferguson, Keith Ferrari, Joan Field, Jeremy Fine, Peter Finn, Stephen Fitzalan, Christian Fletcher, Ray Flight, Patrick Ford, Gary Forecast, Terry Forrestal, Sally Fox, Robert Frank, Kathleen Fraser, Iris Fry, Ricky Galahad, Paul Galloway, Caron Gardner, Martin Garfield, Jo Gibson, Alec Gifford, Kenneth Gilbert, Donald Gilbey, Ann Gilliam, George Gilmour, Alan Gold, Laurie Goode, Carole Anne Goodman, Pat Gorman, Paul Govas, Lynn Gray, Anita Green, Jan Griffiths, Elizabeth Gronow, Trevor St. John Hacker, Adrian Hammond, Dave Hampson, Mike Harris, Paul Harris, Jean Hastings, Cassie Hatton, Glen Hayes, Ken Hazeldine, Aaron Heard, Gabrielle Hecht, Nick Helder, Judy Herbert, Andy Herrity, Tom Hibbert, George Higgins, Kit Hillier, Lew Hooper, Dick Hope, Clive Hopkins, Vivianne Horne, Clive Hurst, Philip Ingham, Paul Irving, Harry Isaacs, Jason Ives, Juliette James, Tex James, Charles Jiminez, Joanne

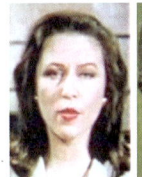
Kate Ricketts

Erika Hoffman

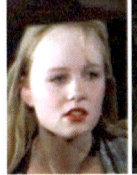
Emma Bunton

Lucy Parker

Paula Terry

Anthony Smee

Soo Drouet

Guest 1

Guest 2

Guest 3

Guest 4

Guest 5

Johnstone, Barrie Jones, Cori Josias, Simon Kane, Michael Kaufman, Rick Kennedy, Mike Kent, Paul Kirby, Harry Klein, Francesca Lacey, Penny Lambirth, Barbara Lampshire, Terra Landers, Paul Langley, Lisa Law, Ken Lawrie, Pat LeClerc, Irene Leigh, Debbie Lloyd, Roger Low, Don McLean, Della McRae, Ben Mansworth, Paul Markham, Ronald Markham, John Marley, Raymond Martin, Tina Maskell, Stephen Mason, Ken Mercer, Lawrence Merry, Nicola Miles, Ellen Miller, George Miller, Richard Moody, Brian Moorehead, Brian Morgan-Carter, Dermot Mulqueen, Mike Mungarvan, Jonathan Murray, Stuart Myers, Nilar Myin, Frank Neary, Clive Norman, Cliffe Obaseki, Kevin O'Brien, Rowland Ogden, Mick Oliver, Mark O'Reilly, Lisa Page, Gabrielle Parker, Alisdair Paul, Sarah Perkins, Ray Pollington, Theo Pouros, Brychan Powell, Huw Prall, Ken Pritchard, Paul Puig, Susan Raasay, Prudence Ren-

House Functionary

M.P.

Young Guy 1

Young Guy 2

nick, Steve Rickard, Kevin Ryan, Simon Sands, Roy Seeley, John Sergeant, Carol Shaw, Larry Sheppard, Julian Sherman, Sally Sinclair, Graham Skidmore, Anthony Smee, Barbara Smith, Anthony Snell, Guy Standeven, Douglas Stark, Sarah-Jane Stedman, David Steele, Bernice Stegers, Graham Stevens, Kerry Stokes, Barry Summerford, Al Szucs, Dean Taylor, Kim Taylor, Andy Thompson, Clive Thompson, Mal Tobias, Cy Town, Frank Tregear, Felicity Trew, Kathryn Turner, Roger Turner, Marcus Tylor, Chris Underhill, Alan Uttley-Moore, Derek Van Weenen, Paul Vincent, Tricia Vincent, Sheila

Vivien, Kelvin Warren, Jeff Whitfield, Alan Wicks, Danny Wilder, Renee Williams, Wayne, Paul Weakley, Maxine Weavers, Kate Webb, Tony Winn, Tina Winter, Leslie Weekes, Joe Wells, Joe Tommy Winward, Andrew Wenborne, June West, Ken Woodman, Arnold Zarom

Still haunted by the murder of Mattie Storin, Francis Urquhart addresses the camera, saying "It had to be done. It's in the past. It's over."

Ian Richardson on the stairs

Leonard Preston makes a speech

In his ongoing battle with the King, Urquhart decides to call an election and has senior party members and his new adviser Sarah Harding spend the weekend at Chequers.

Bernice Stegers, Frederick Treves

David Ryall, Bernice Stegers

Kitty Aldridge, Ian Richardson

Ian Richardson, Kitty Aldridge, Colin Jeavons

He names Chief Whip Tim Stamper party chairman but is somewhat reticent at making any post-election promises. The King also decides to go on the offensive.

The House of Commons

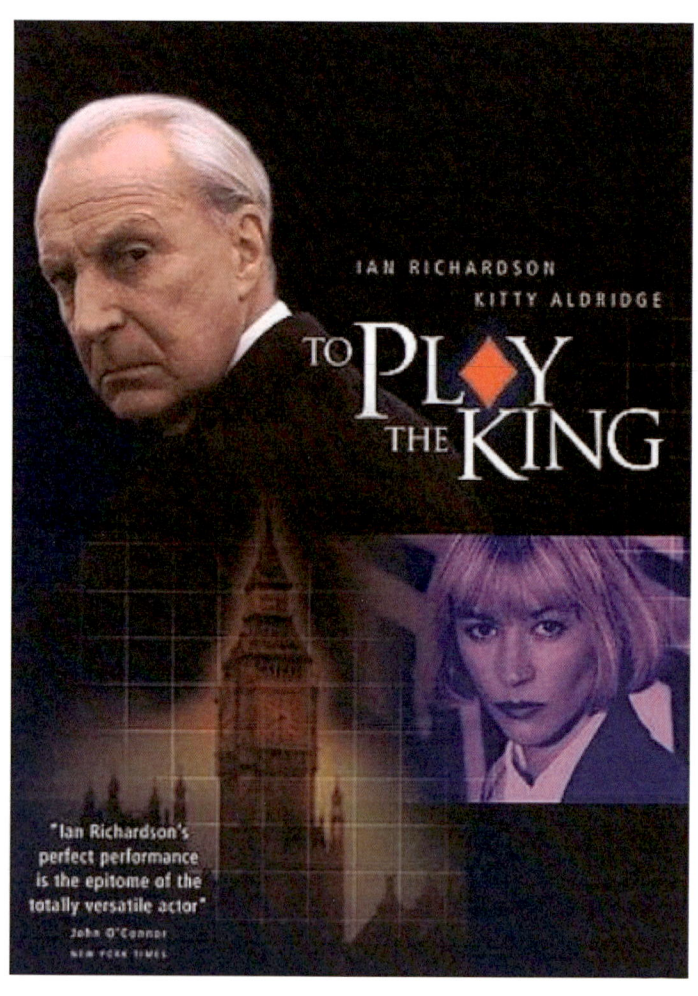

Television Poster

He plans a television documentary where he will again push his views on the need for a compassionate, caring society. Sarah arranges for a poll favorable to the government.

Having separated from his wife, the King's chief of staff and press secretary, David Mycroft, has found new interests in the form of a handsome man. Walking down the street alone, Sarah is accosted and told to ask the PM about Mattie Storin.

Colin Jeavons, George Raistrick

Leonard Preston, Elizabeth Chambers

Diane Fletcher, Ian Richardson

Michael Kitchen, Rowena King

Meanwhile David Mycroft is still staying at the home of his new boyfriend, Ken Charterhouse. He tells Ken that he is actually Press Secretary and Chief of Staff at Buckingham Palace.

Ian Richardson dressing

During a dinner given by the King for some of the cabinet members, bombs go off; Corder tells Urquhart that the I.R.A. should get the blame, which appeals to the P.M.

Michael Kitchen, Nicholas Farrell, Rowena King

Nicholas Farrell, Jack Fortune

Christopher Owen, Kenneth Gilbert

John Stroud then asks a question in the House as to whether the three citizens of the Irish Republic shot dead at a shopping centre by order of the Prime Minister.

Two young poofs at the club

Ian Richardson, Michael Kitchen

Urquhart et al on the bench

Urquhart quotes the Official Secret Act, while John Staines stands up and says that they should be grateful to Urquhart for getting rid of terrorists, not censure him.

Later, a couple of poofs recognize Mycroft at a club, saying they will keep his secret. Sarah asks Francis about Mattie Storin; he gives her a believable explanation of his involvement with her.

Anthony Smee makes a speech

TO PLAY THE KING EPISODE 3

DIRECTED BY Paul Seed
ORIGINAL AIR DATE: 12/5/93

CAST

Ian Richardson.........Francis Urquhart
Michael Kitchen..........................King
Kitty Aldridge..............Sarah Harding
Colin Jeavons.................Tim Stamper
Diane Fletcher......Elizabeth Urquhart
Nicholas Farrell...........David Mycroft
Rowena King.........Chloe Carmichael
Bernice Stegers......Princess Charlotte
David Ryall...........Sir Bruce Bullerby
John Bird..........Brian Brynford-Jones
Leonard Preston...............John Stroud
Jack Fortune...........Ken Charterhouse
Frederick Treves......Lord Quillington
Pip Torrens...............Andrew Harding
Anthony Smee................John Staines
Nick Brimble..........................Corder
William Chubb...........John Krajewski
Merelina Kendall....Hilda Cordwainer
Don Warrington...........Graham Gaunt
James Snell......................D.I. Hackett
Erika Hoffman....................The Lady

Ian Richardson

Michael Kitchen

Kitty Aldridge

Colin Jeavons

Diane Fletcher

Nicholas Farrell

Rowena King

Bernice Stegers

Tacy Kneale...........................Solicitor
Paula Tilbrook........................Speaker
John Bleasdale......Sardonic Journalist
Richard Trice...............................PPS
Jeremy Clyne............................Editor
Ti Heath......................Male Secretary
Tom Beasley.................Young Prince
Susannah Harker............Mattie Storin
Ken Coombs..............Home Secretary
Ryan Hurst...........................Page Boy

David Ryall

John Bird

Leonard Preston

Jack Fortune

Frederick Treves

Pip Torrens

Anthony Smee

Nick Brimble

William Chubb

Don Warrington

James Snell

Erika Hoffman

AND: Michael Ackerman, David Adams, Kitty Aldridge, Dane Alexander, Mark Allington, Lee Alliston, Miles Ambrose, David Arnold, Richard Ashley, Jackie Avey, Fiona Baker, Micky Baker, Rosemary Banks, Jackie Barnes, Andy Barrett, Julian Barsham, Adrian Bell, Andrew Bell, Simon Bell, Adrian Bennett, Gary Bentley, June Bernice, David Billa, Ezra Bix, Judith Blakstad, George Blee, Jane Bough, Willy Bowman, Ray Boyd, Mark Brett, Annie Bright, Mervyn Brooker, Ingrid Bradley, James Bulbeck, Tina Bunnag, Nick Burgess, Sophie Burnham, Patricia Butler, Roy Byrne, Woolf Byrne, Yvonne Byrne, Graham Carrigan, Guy Carter, Graham Case, Con Chambers, Elizabeth Chambers, Jean Channon, Mark Chapman, William Chubb, Melita Clarke, Trisha Clarke, Helena Clayton, John

Clements, Michael Cole, Mair Coleman, Judy Collins, Keith Connolly, Peter Cooney, June Cooper, Malcolm Cooper, Judy Cowne, Pamela Craine, Derek Currell, Paul Dark, John Darling, Cyril Davey, Tom Deluvian, Terrance Denville, Serena Destouche, John Dodd, Chris Dyson, Ian Easton, Jon Fedyk, Sybil Ferguson, Keith Ferrari, Joan Field, Jeremy Fine, Peter Finn, Stephen Fitzalan, Christian Fletcher, Ray Flight, Patrick Ford, Gary Forecast, Terry Forrestal, Sally Fox, Robert Frank, Kathleen Fraser, Iris Fry, Ricky Galahad, Paul Galloway, Caron Gardner, Martin Garfield, Jo Gibson, Alec Gifford, Kenneth Gilbert, Donald Gilbey, Ann Gilliam, George Gilmour, Alan Gold, Laurie Goode, Carole Anne Goodman, Pat Gorman, Paul Govas, Lynn Gray, Anita Green, Jan Griffiths, Elizabeth Gronow, Trevor St. John Hacker, Adrian Hammond, Dave Hampson, Mike Harris, Paul Harris, Jean Hastings, Cassie Hat-

Tacy Kneale

John Bleasdal

Richard Trice

Jeremy Clyne

Tom Beasley   Ken Coombs

ton, Glen Hayes, Ken Hazeldine, Aaron Heard, Gabrielle Hecht, Nick Helder, Judy Herbert, Andy Herrity, Tom Hibbert, George Higgins, Kit Hillier, Lew Hooper, Dick Hope, Clive Hopkins, Vivianne Horne, Clive Hurst, Philip Ingham, Paul Irving, Harry Isaacs, Jason Ives, Juliette James, Tex James, Charles Jiminez, Joanne Johnstone, Barrie Jones, Cori Josias, Simon Kane, Michael Kaufman, Rick Kennedy, Mike Kent, Paul Kirby, Harry Klein, Francesca Lacey, Penny Lambirth, Barbara Lampshire, Terra Landers, Paul Langley, Lisa Law, Ken Lawrie, Pat LeClerc, Irene Leigh, Debbie Lloyd, Roger Low, Don McLean, Della McRae, Ben Mansworth, Paul Markham, Ronald Markham, John Marley, Raymond Martin, Tina Maskell, Stephen Mason, Ken Mercer, Lawrence Merry, Nicola Miles, Ellen Miller, George Miller, Richard Moody, Brian Moorehead, Brian Morgan-Carter, Dermot Mulqueen, Mike Mungarvan, Jonathan Murray, Stuart Myers, Nilar Myin, Frank Neary, Clive Norman, Cliffe Obaseki, Kevin O'Brien, Rowland Ogden, Mick Oliver, Mark O'Reilly, Lisa Page, Gabrielle Parker, Alisdair Paul, Sarah Perkins, Ray Pollington, Theo Pouros, Brychan Powell, Huw Prall, Ken Pritchard, Paul Puig, Susan Raasay, Prudence Rennick, Steve Rickard, Kevin Ryan, Simon Sands, Roy Seeley, John Sergeant, Carol Shaw, Larry Sheppard, Julian Sherman, Sally Sinclair, Graham Skidmore, Anthony Smee, Barbara Smith, Anthony Snell, Guy Standeven, Douglas Stark, Sarah-Jane Stedman, David Steele, Bernice Stegers, Graham Stevens, Kerry Stokes, Barry Summerford, Al Szucs, Dean Taylor, Kim Taylor, Andy Thompson, Clive Thompson, Mal Tobias, Cy Town, Frank Tregear, Felicity Trew, Kathryn Turner, Roger Turner, Marcus Tylor, Chris Underhill, Alan Uttley-Moore, Derek Van Weenen, Paul Vincent, Tricia Vincent, Sheila Vivien, Kelvin Warren, Jeff Wayne, Paul Weakley, Maxine Weavers, Kate Webb, Leslie Weekes, Joe Wells, Joe Wenborne, June West, Ken Whitfield, Alan Wicks, Danny Wilder, Renee Williams, Tony Winn, Tina Winter, Tommy Winward, Andrew Woodman, Arnold Zarom

Despite his pleas to the King to avoid a constitutional crisis and not publicly express his personal views, the King refuses and Urquhart decides to destroy him.

Ian Richardson at his desk

Jeremy Clyne, David Ryall

Anthony Smee, Tacy Kneale

TV Poster

Princess Charlotte begins dictating her memoirs and also sleeping with publisher Sir Bruce Bullerby. She has a lot to tell about the Royal Family.

As planned, the King goes on television and the program is seen as a clear attack on the government. Urqhart has seriously underestimated the King's influence and the party finds itself falling in the polls.

Don Warrington giving the news

Ian Richardson on the phone

When a conservative M.P., John Staines, is arrested by the police for child molestation, David Mycroft is worried that his own lifestyle choice-which does not include underage minors- will become public and embarrass the King.

Colin Jeavons, Richard Trice

Colin Jeavons, Ian Richardson

Sarah gets a threatening phone call and meets Mattie Storin's friend John Krajewski to find out what he thinks really happened to her. He thinks Mattie was killed on Urquhart's orders-and is sure Urquhart laced Roger O'Neill's cocaine with rat poison.

Erika Hoffman as the Lady

Ian Richardson, Kitty Aldridge

Meanwhile, Francis Urquhart goes to the House for Prime Minister's question time. "Very frightening," he says sarcastically. "It's like being mugged by a guinea pig."

118

Rowena King, Nicholas Farrell

Ken Coombs, Ian Richardson

Urquhart is very upset when he learns that Staines made an impassioned speech in the House of Commons rebuffing recent attacks on the government just before he was arrested.

Clarion headline

Bernice Stegers, David Ryall

Nick Brimble, Ian Richardson

The speech criticized the lifestyles of the aristocracy-as well as the royal family. Urquhart says it was a good speech; too bad it will not carry the same moral weight now.

Kitty Aldridge, Pip Torrens

Rowena King, Nicholas Farrell

Colin Jeavons, Ian Richardson

David Ryall, Ian Richardson

When Sarah's husband Andrew discovers that she is having an affair with Francis Urquhart, he calls her a selfish bitch, demanding she call off the affair. She won't do it.

Urquhart calls Bullerby into his office demanding that he publish Charlotte's memoirs now, not after her death as agreed. When shown pictures of himself naked on top of Charlotte, Bullerby agrees.

Urquhart in the House

TO PLAY THE KING EPISODE 4

DIRECTED BY Paul Seed
ORIGINAL AIR DATE: 11/12/93

CAST

Ian Richardson.........Francis Urquhart
Michael Kitchen..........................King
Kitty Aldridge..............Sarah Harding
Colin Jeavons.................Tim Stamper
Diane Fletcher......Elizabeth Urquhart
Nicholas Farrell...........David Mycroft
Rowena King.........Chloe Carmichael
Leonard Preston...............John Stroud
Jack Fortune...........Ken Charterhouse
Erika Hoffman.....................The Lady
Nick Brimble...........................Corder
Richard Howard..............John Sarkey
Richard Durden...........B.B.C. Official
Kate Ricketts.....Current Affairs Lady
Geoffrey McGivern.....Bill Rochester
Adam Bareham.................Interviewer
John Paul Connolly......Sturdy Beggar
Don Warrington...........Graham Gaunt
Angus Kennedy...........Court Reporter
Stanley Finni....................Chloe's Pet
Declan Skeete....................New Rasta

Ian Richardson

Michael Kitchen

Kitty Aldridge

Colin Jeavons

Diane Fletcher

Nicholas Farrell

Rowena King

Leonard Preston

```
Julian Harries...................Para Officer
Tom Karol......................TV Presenter
Prudence Rennick................Mayoress
Lawrence Werber....Returning Officer
Tom Beasley....................Young King
Susannah Harker............Mattie Storin
Ryan Hurst...........................Page Boy
```

Jack Fortune

Erika Hoffman

AND: Michael Ackerman, David Adams, Kitty Aldridge, Dane Alexander, Mark Allington, Lee Alliston, Miles Ambrose, David Arnold, Richard Ashley, Jackie Avey, Fiona Baker, Micky Baker, Rosemary Banks, Jackie Barnes, Andy Barrett, Julian Barsham, Adrian Bell, Andrew Bell, Simon Bell, Adrian Bennett, Gary Bentley, June Bernice, David Billa, Ezra Bix, Judith Blakstad, George Blee, Jane Bough, Willy Bowman, Ray Boyd, Mark Brett, Annie Bright, Mervyn Brooker, Ingrid Bradley, James Bulbeck, Tina Bunnag, Nick Burgess, Sophie Burnham, Patricia Butler, Roy Byrne, Woolf Byrne, Yvonne Byrne, Graham Carrigan, Guy Carter, Graham Case, Con Chambers, Elizabeth Chambers, Jean Channon, Mark Chapman, William Chubb, Melita Clarke, Trisha Clarke, Helena Clayton, John Clements, Michael Cole, Mair Coleman, Judy Collins, Keith Connolly, Peter Cooney, June Cooper, Malcolm Cooper, Judy Cowne, Pamela Craine, Der-

Nick Brimble

Richard Howard

Richard Durden

Kate Ricketts

Geoffrey McGivern

John Paul Connolly

Don Warrington

Stanley Finni Stanley Finni

Julian Harries

Tom Karol

ek Currell, Paul Dark, John Darling, Cyril Davey, Tom Deluvian, Terrance Denville, Serena Destouche, John Dodd, Chris Dyson, Ian Easton, Jon Fedyk, Sybil Ferguson, Keith Ferrari, Joan Field, Jeremy Fine, Peter Finn, Stephen Fitzalan, Christian Fletcher, Ray Flight, Patrick Ford, Gary Forecast, Terry Forrestal, Sally Fox, Robert Frank, Kathleen Fraser, Iris Fry, Ricky Galahad, Paul Galloway, Caron Gardner, Martin Garfield, Jo Gibson, Alec Gifford, Kenneth Gilbert, Donald Gilbey, Ann Gilliam, George Gilmour, Alan Gold, Laurie Goode, Carole Anne Goodman, Pat Gorman, Paul Govas, Lynn Gray, Anita Green, Jan Griffiths, Elizabeth Gronow, Trevor St. John Hacker, Adrian Hammond, Dave Hampson, Mike Harris, Paul Harris, Jean Hastings, Cassie Hatton, Glen Hayes, Ken Hazeldine, Aaron Heard, Gabrielle Hecht, Nick Helder, Judy Herbert, Andy Herrity, Tom Hibbert, George Higgins, Kit Hillier, Lew Hooper, Dick Hope, Clive Hopkins, Vivianne Horne, Clive Hurst, Philip Ingham, Paul Irving, Harry Isaacs, Jason Ives, Juliette James, Tex James, Charles Jiminez, Joanne Johnstone, Barrie Jones, Cori Josias, Simon Kane, Michael Kaufman, Rick Kennedy, Mike Kent, Paul Kirby, Harry Klein, Francesca Lacey, Penny Lam-

Prudence Rennick

Lawrence Werber

Tom Beasley

Black Woman 1

Black Woman 2

Gunman

Minister

Newsman

Palace Butler

Reporter 1

Reporter 2

Reporter 3

127

birth, Barbara Lampshire, Terra Landers, Paul Langley, Lisa Law, Ken Lawrie, Pat LeClerc, Irene Leigh, Debbie Lloyd, Roger Low, Don McLean, Della McRae, Ben Mansworth, Paul Markham, Ronald Markham, John Marley, Raymond Martin, Tina Maskell, Stephen Mason, Ken Mercer, Lawrence Merry, Nicola Miles, Ellen Miller, George Miller, Richard Moody, Brian Moorehead, Brian Morgan-Carter, Dermot Mulqueen, Mike Mungarvan, Jonathan Murray, Stuart Myers, Nilar Myin, Frank Neary, Clive Norman, Cliffe Obaseki, Kevin O'Brien, Rowland Ogden, Mick Oliver, Mark O'Reilly, Lisa Page, Gabrielle Parker, Alisdair Paul, Sarah Perkins, Ray Pollington, Theo Pouros, Brychan Powell, Huw Prall, Ken Pritchard, Paul Puig, Susan Raasay, Prudence Rennick, Steve Rickard, Kevin Ryan, Simon Sands, Roy Seeley, John Sergeant, Carol Shaw, Larry Sheppard, Julian Sherman, Sally Sinclair, Graham Skidmore, Anthony

Reporter 4   Thug

Smee, Barbara Smith, Anthony Snell, Guy Standeven, Douglas Stark, Sarah-Jane Stedman, David Steele, Bernice Stegers, Graham Stevens, Kerry Stokes, Barry Summerford, Al Szucs, Dean Taylor, Kim Taylor, Andy Thompson, Clive Thompson, Mal Tobias, Cy Town, Frank Tregear, Felicity Trew, Kathryn Turner, Roger Turner, Marcus Tylor, Chris Underhill, Alan Uttley-Moore, Derek Van Weenen, Paul Vincent, Tricia Vincent, Sheila Vivien, Kelvin Warren, Jeff Wayne, Paul Weakley, Maxine Weavers, Kate Webb, Leslie Weekes, Joe Wells, Joe Wenborne, June West, Ken Whitfield, Alan Wicks, Danny Wilder, Renee Williams, Tony Winn, Tina Winter, Tommy Winward, Andrew Woodman, Arnold Zarom

Francis Urquhart calls the election but the party is down 13 points in the polls and he will obviously have a hard slog ahead if he is to be reelected.

Rowena King, Nicholas Farrell

Nicholas Farrell as David Mycroft

Michael Kitchen, Ian Richardson

Nicholas Farrell, Michael Kitchen

Michael Kitchen, Ian Richardson

Nick Brimble, Diane Fletcher, Ian Richardson

Nicholas Farrell, Rowena King

A gas explosion in a block of flats gives the King a platform to drive home his point about the need to invest more in housing and social services, but the P.M. also makes use of the opportunity to remind the King to stay out of politics.

Party Chairman Tim Stamper is not very pleased that his old friend Urquhart won't promise him a senior Cabinet post should they win the election and he sets out to ruin him.

Diane Fletcher, Ian Richardson

Julian Harries on the attack

Ian Richardson, Kitty Aldridge

Stanley Finni, Rowena King

As the Conservative party inches ever closer to being reelected, Urquhart must deal with Stamper and Sarah, both of whom have the evidence to bring him down.

Urquhart arranges for Corder to have the King abducted by thugs during his tour of a Manchester estate; the military was following the King on Urquhart's orders, rescuing him from possible harm.

Urquhart on the news

Tom Karol, Ian Richardson

TV Poster

The King is seen as foolish for his negligence in the matter of security, and Urquhart seems like a hero for having protected him.

Meanwhile, Corder discovers that Stamper has passed information on Mattie Storin's murder to a journalist as insurance. With urging from his wife Elizabeth, Urquhart orders Corder to assassinate them. Their deaths are put down to the I.R.A.

Tom Beasley, Erika Hoffman

The King on the news

Ian Richardson, Kitty Aldridge, Colin Jeavons

Ian Richardson as Francis Urquhart

The Conservatives subsequently win the general election with a 22-seat overall majority. With his policies vindicated by the electorate, despite the King's public opposition, Urquhart demands his abdication.

The new teenaged King is crowned, showing that Urquhart had succeeded in obtaining the abdication of the previous king. Urquhart grins at the camera and says "God save the King."

The Urquharts at the long table

Everyone is being taped!

THE FINAL CUT EPISODE 1

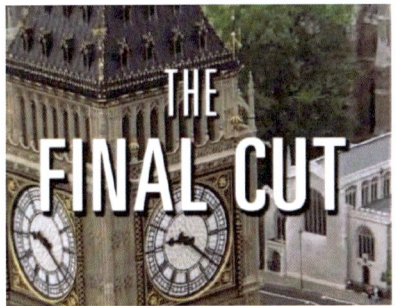

DIRECTED BY Mike Vardy
ORIGINAL AIR DATE: 11/5/95

CAST

Ian Richardson.........Francis Urquhart
Diane Fletcher......Elizabeth Urquhart
Paul Freeman............Tom Makepeace
Isla Blair.......................Claire Carlsen
Nickolas Grace...Geoffrey Booza Pitt
Kevork Malikyan......................Nures
David Ryall...........Sir Bruce Bullerby
Julian Fellowes...Sir Henry Ponsonby
Muriel Pavlow......Age Concern Lady
John Rowe..............Sir Clive Watling
Glyn Grain......................John Rayner
Nick Brimble...........................Corder
Alison Peebles..............Betsy Bourne
Cherith Mellor.......Hilary Makepeace
William Scott-Masson...Barry Crumb
Andrew Seear.............Michael Wolfin
Peter Symonds.......................Polecutt
Dorothy Vernon.......................Speaker
Erika Hoffman.......................Princess
Ian Mercer.....................Graham Glass
Tom Beasley....................Young King

Ian Richardson

Diane Fletcher

Paul Freeman

Isla Blair

Nickolas Grace

Kevork Malikyan

David Ryall

Julian Fellowes

Duggie Brown...................Joe Badger
Richard Bebb..Political Commentator
Lynne Verrall.............................Nurse
Gwendolyn Watts........Sturdy Woman
Sue Edelson......................Newsreader
Trevor Steedman..................Detective
Susannah Harker............Mattie Storin
Jim McCahy.................U.S. President
Reg Thomason...Man Singing Happy Birthday
Marc Cass, Derek Lea, Ray Nicholas
..................................Motorway Thugs

Muriel Pavlow   John Rowe

Glyn Grain   Nick Brimble

Alison Peebles   Cherith Mellor

William Scott-Masson   Andrew Seear

Peter Symonds   Erika Hoffman

Ian Mercer   Tom Beasley

AND: Angela Abrahams, Michael Ackerman, Margaret Alderman, Kitty Aldridge, Jerry Baker, Micky Baker, Mitch Barber, Ann Barrass, Julian Barsham, Paul Barton, Helen Beckman, Lisette Bell-Simmonds, Sacha Bennett, Gerald Benson, Hazel Birrell, Jane Bishop, Judith Blackstad, George Blee, Jane Bough, Andrew Bowen, Willy Bowman, Raymond Boyd, Mark Brett, Pam Buckley, Ray Burdis, Ron Burrage, Janine Button, Roy Byrne, Woolf Byrne, Carol Careford, Giovanni Caruso, Marc Cass, Ray Chaney, Mark Chapman, Nick Chapman, Claire Chrysler, Melita Clarke, Trisha Clarke, John Clements, Val Clover, Samara Cohen, Freddie Comrie, Ken Coombs, Malcolm Cooper, Lynn Costenbarder, Alan Crisp, Bert Crome, Barry Davey, Cyril Davey, Malcolm Davey, Lionel De Clerc,

John Denton, Sharton Douglas, Carlos Duque, Chris Dyson, George Ensor, Geoffrey Evans, Susan Farthing, David Field, Joan Field, Neill Finnighan, Juliet Forester, Salo Gardner, Martin Garfield, David Garry, Barry Gay, Andy Gell, Helen Georgette, Selena Gilbert, Anthony Gilding, George Gilmour, Laurie Goode, Brian Goodwin, Pat Gorman, Anita Green, Charles Grima, Adrian Hammond, Paul Harris, Cassie Hatton, Tom Hibbert, George Higgins, Dick Hope, Elaine Hopkins, Mex Horne, Ted Houser, Derek Hunt, Philip Ingham, Eric Jack, Jessica James, Juliette James, Leonie Jessel, Dianne Kelly, Michael Kennedy, Mark Kirby, Paul Kirby, Joe Lacey, Penny Lambirth, Pat LeClerc, Aileen Lewis, Alex Lewis, Derek Lyons, Robert McGibbon, Alison McGuire, Steve Marco, Sergio Marini, Colin Martin, Raymond Martin, Tina Maskell, Anna Mattina, Mary Maxted, Erol Mehmet, Richard Moody, Brian Moorehead, Stephen Morphew, Mike Morrell, Mike Mungarvan, Stuart Myers, Ray Nicholas, Clive Norman, Mimi Novic, Gary O'Brien, Kevin O'Brien, Robert Pearson, Andreas Petrides, Philip Phedonos, Carolyn Poole, Theo Pouros, Kaye Power-McGowan, Paul Puig, Celia Radband, Mike Randall, Leslie Rhodes, Ray Riches, Steve Rickard,

Duggie Brown

Lynne Verrall

Sue Edelson   Trevor Steedman

Reg Thomason

Marc Cass

Derek Lea

Ray Nicholas

Attendant

Carlsen

Constable

Dog

Denise Ryan, Paul Salt, Simon Sands, Terry Sartain, Daphne Selfe, John Sergent, Molly Seyforth, Carol Shaw, Ted Shepherd, Larry Sheppard, Sally Sinclair, Rodney Smith, Guy Standeven, Douglas Stark, Trevor Steedman, Graham Stevens, Keith Swaden, Joe Szucs, Vanessa Taverner, Colin Thomas, Mal Tobias, Cy Town, Edwin Ubels, Alan Uttley-Moore, Harry Van Engel, Jennifer Van Engel, Ethel Vawdrey, Paul Vincent, Linn Waldegrave, Leslie Weekes, Howard Whiteson, Kim Whitfield, Eddie Whiting, Alan Wicks, Nick Wilkinson, Tony Winn, Brian Winsor, Peter Zander

Elderly Woman   M.P. 1

M.P. 2   M.P. 3

Sarah   Young Cypriot 1

Young Cypriot 2

Approaching his 65th birthday, Prime Minister Frances Urquhart begins to see the end of his career. Not that he has the intention of resigning anytime soon.

He does however hope to establish a legacy, one for the history books and one to provide his pension. For the latter, his wife Elizabeth introduces him to Mr. Nures, a Turkish-Cypriot businessman.

Julian Fellowes, Nick Brimble

Police taking aim at the hoodlums

Nures will contribute handsomely to the Urquhart Trust if the upcoming boundary commission report provides a ruling favorable to Turkish-occupied Cyprus.

Ian Richardson, John Rowe, Julian Fellowes

Diane Fletcher, Julian Fellowes

Diane Fletcher, Ian Richardson

Diane Fletcher, Kevork Malikyan

English cricket match

Ian Richardson, Diane Fletcher, Kevork Malikyan

Nures says that he is grateful to Urquhart for creating a climate for which a man of vision can express himself to the full. England is the best country in the world for the merchant adventurer.

Andrew Seear, Glyn Grain

Paul Freeman, Ian Richardson Isla Blair

As for the history books, Francis has decided to take credit for the upcoming peace deal in Cyprus, much to the consternation of the Foreign Secretary, Tom Makepeace.

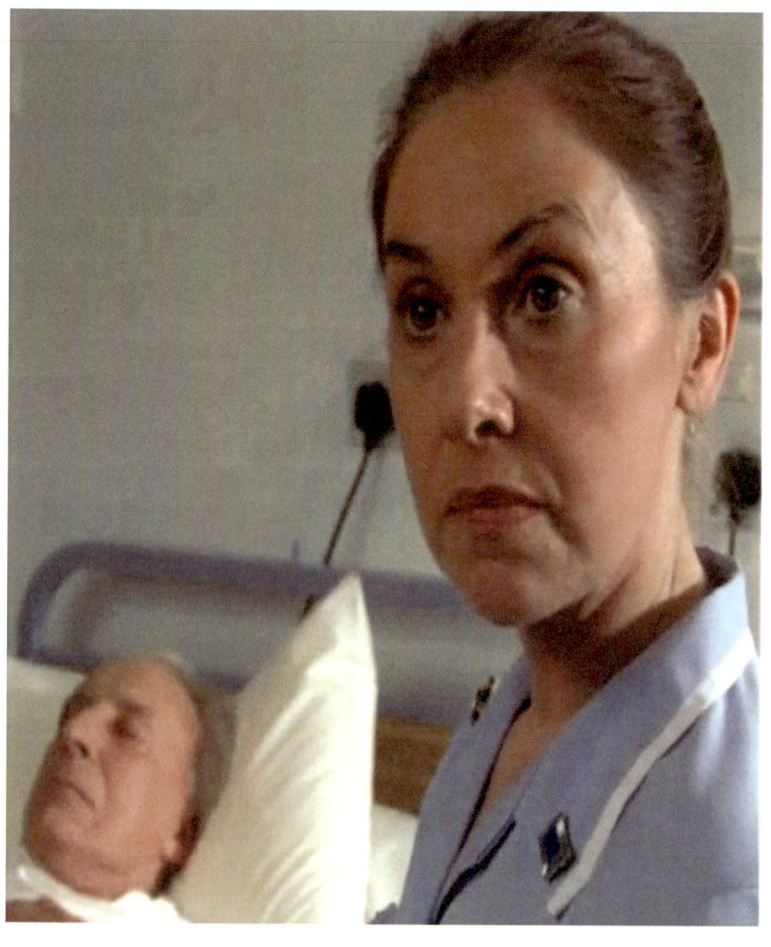

Ian Richardson, Lynne Verrall

Diane Fletcher, Ian Richardson

Reg Thomas, Muriel Pavlow et al

However, in his House speech, Urquhart thanks Makepeace for his hard-working part in bringing together the deal, having been "loaded down with much of the donkey work." Makepeace considers this insulting.

Nickolas Grace, Ian Richardson, Andrew Seear

Julian Fellowes, Ian Richardson

Glyn Grain, Paul Freeman

Returning to London on the motorway from a meeting with the oil company executive, Urquhart's car is rammed by another car containing three drunken louts. The attackers are quickly shot dead by his security staff.

Urquhart sustains minor head injuries in the collision, but his life is not endangered. Recovering in his hospital room, Urquhart experiences again his recurring nightmare about the killings in Cyprus.

Ian Richardson, Constable

Peter Symonds, Andrew Seear

Nickolas Grace, Ian Richardson

When Elizabeth arrives at the hospital, he is delirious and confuses the incident on the motorway with the incident in Cyprus.

Deputy P.M. Tom Makepeace chairs a cabinet meeting while Urquhart is in hospital, and it is announced that the motorway incident was simply the result of "road rage."

Urquhart considers Makepeace as a potential challenger, although he doesn't take the threat very seriously, considering him "not a fighter" but "a sentimental dreamer."

Erika Hoffman, Tom Beasley

THE FINAL CUT EPISODE 2

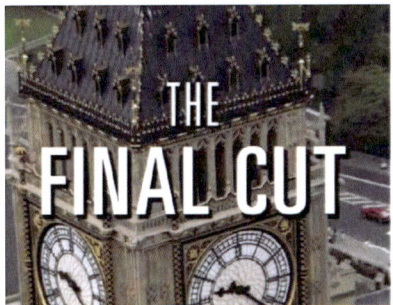

DIRECTED BY Mike Vardy
ORIGINAL AIR DATE: 11/12/95

CAST

Ian Richardson.........Francis Urquhart
Diane Fletcher......Elizabeth Urquhart
Paul Freeman............Tom Makepeace
Isla Blair.......................Claire Carlsen
Nickolas Grace...Geoffrey Booza Pitt
Yolanda Vazquez......Maria Passolides
Leon Lissek....Evanghelos Passolides
John Rowe...............Sir Clive Watling
Glyn Grain.......................John Rayner
Nick Brimble...........................Corder
Andrew Seear............Michael Wolfin
Bunny May.................................Clerk
Peter Symonds......................Polecutt
Dorothy Vernon.......................Speaker
Duggie Brown...................Joe Badger
Michael Wardle.................Hugh Pugh
Nicholas Blane.............Dicky Withers
John Langford.................TV Reporter
Carole Copeland......Woman Reporter

AND: Angela Abrahams, Michael

Ian Richardson

Diane Fletcher

Paul Freeman

Isla Blair

Nickolas Grace

Yolanda Vazquez

Leon Lissek

John Rowe

Ackerman, Margaret Alderman, Kitty
Aldridge, Jerry Baker, Micky Baker,
Mitch Barber, Ann Barrass, Julian
Barsham, Paul Barton, Helen Beck-
man, Lisette Bell-Simmonds, Sa-
cha Bennett, Gerald Benson, Hazel
Birrell, Jane Bishop, Judith Blackstad,
George Blee, Jane Bough, Andrew
Bowen, Willy Bowman, Raymond
Boyd, Mark Brett, Pam Buckley, Ray
Burdis, Ron Burrage, Janine Button,
Roy Byrne, Woolf Byrne, Carol Car-
eford, Giovanni Caruso, Marc Cass,
Ray Chaney, Mark Chapman, Nick
Chapman, Claire Chrysler, Melita
Clarke, Trisha Clarke, John Clements,
Val Clover, Samara Cohen, Freddie
Comrie, Ken Coombs, Malcolm Coo-
per, Lynn Costenbarder, Alan Crisp,
Bert Crome, Barry Davey, Cyril Dav-
ey, Malcolm Davey, Lionel De Clerc,
John Denton, Sharton Douglas, Car-
los Duque, Chris Dyson, George En-
sor, Geoffrey Evans, Susan Farthing,
David Field, Joan Field, Neill Finni-
ghan, Juliet Forester, Salo Gardner,
Martin Garfield, David Garry, Barry
Gay, Andy Gell, Helen Georgette,
Selena Gilbert, Anthony Gilding,
George Gilmour, Laurie Goode,
Brian Goodwin, Pat Gorman, Anita
Green, Charles Grima, Adrian Ham-
mond, Paul Harris, Cassie Hatton,
Tom Hibbert, George Higgins, Dick

Glyn Grain

Nick Brimble

Andrew Seear

Bunny May

Peter Symonds

Duggie Brown

Michael Wardle

Nicholas Blane

John Langford

Carole Copeland

M.P. 1

M.P. 2

Hope, Elaine Hopkins, Mex Horne, Ted Houser, Derek Hunt, Philip Ingham, Eric Jack, Jessica James, Juliette James, Leonie Jessel, Dianne Kelly, Michael Kennedy, Mark Kirby, Paul Kirby, Joe Lacey, Penny Lambirth, Pat LeClerc, Aileen Lewis, Alex Lewis, Derek Lyons, Robert McGibbon, Alison McGuire, Steve Marco, Sergio Marini, Colin Martin, Raymond Martin, Tina Maskell, Anna Mattina, Mary Maxted, Erol Mehmet, Richard Moody, Brian Moorehead, Stephen Morphew, Mike Morrell, Mike Mungarvan, Stuart Myers, Ray Nicholas, Clive Norman, Mimi Novic, Gary O'Brien, Kevin O'Brien, Robert Pearson, Andreas Petrides, Philip Phedonos, Carolyn Poole, Theo Pouros, Kaye Power-McGowan, Paul Puig, Celia Radband, Mike Randall, Leslie Rhodes, Ray Riches, Steve Rickard, Denise Ryan, Paul Salt, Simon Sands, Terry Sartain, Daphne Selfe, John Sergent, Molly Seyforth, Carol Shaw, Ted Shepherd, Larry Shep-

M.P. 3 M.P. 4

Reporter 1 Reporter 2

Spectator 1 Spectator 2

pard, Sally Sinclair, Rodney Smith, Guy Standeven, Douglas Stark, Trevor Steedman, Graham Stevens, Keith Swaden, Joe Szucs, Vanessa Taverner, Colin Thomas, Reg Thomason, Mal Tobias, Cy Town, Edwin Ubels, Alan Uttley-Moore, Harry Van Engel, Jennifer Van Engel, Ethel Vawdrey, Paul Vincent, Linn Waldegrave, Leslie Weekes, Howard Whiteson, Kim Whitfield, Eddie Whiting, Alan Wicks, Nick Wilkinson, Tony Winn, Brian Winsor, Peter Zander

Having sacked his Parliamentary Private Secretary, Urquhart casts about for a replacement. At the suggestion of Geoffrey Booza Pitt he gives serious consideration to backbench MP Claire Carlsen.

Michael Wardle makes a speech

Nickolas Grace, Isla Blair

Yolanda Vazquez, Leon Lissek

Claire is carrying on an affair with Foreign Secretary Tom Makepeace. Claire is clearly playing both sides of the fence to ensure her own place in the hierarchy, regardless of what the future may hold.

Diane Fletcher, Ian Richardson

Peter Symonds, Ian Richardson

Urquhart decides the time has come to shake things up and forces Makepeace to resign, something his wife Elizabeth isn't sure is in their best interest.

Nickolas Grace, Paul Freeman

Diane Fletcher, Ian Richardson

He also continues working on his legacies, dropping a good word in the ear of the British judge on the Cyprus boundary panel.

Isla Blair, Paul Freeman

Diane Fletcher, Nick Brimble

Nickolas Grace, Ian Richardson, Islan Blair

Yolanda Vazquez in the gallery

Meanwhile, the brother of the two Greek Cypriots killed by Urquhart decades ago is now living in London. Unknown to Urquhart, he witnessed their deaths and recognizes Urquhart as the soldier who killed them.

Isla Blair, Nick Brimble

Isla Blair, Nick Brimble, Nickloas Grace

He asks his daughter Maria to investigate, using the pretext that he wishes to find the location where they are buried in order to arrange a proper memorial, but it is revenge rather than mourning that is on his mind.

Paul Freeman announces his resignation

Urquhart in the House

Maria's search of government records finds a report written by the soldier who killed her uncles, but the name of the soldier is deleted. She approaches Urquhart, who appears to be welcoming and eager to help.

Overhead location scene

Andrew Seear, Nickolas Grace, Ian Richardson, Isla Blair

Unknown to her, he arranges that documents revealing his involvement be excluded from a coincidental declassification of records relating to the British involvement in Cyprus. But he also confides the truth to his wife Elizabeth.

Nickolas Grace makes a speech

Ian Richardson on the phone

Urquhart chooses a female protege to replace the indiscreet Geoffrey Booza Pitt. He appoints the ambitious Claire Carlsen as his PPS. Claire also happens to be Makepeace's lover. When Urquhart asks her advice about Makepeace, however, she tells Urquhart to "get rid of him."

Encouraged by Claire, Urquhart enrages Makepeace by making a speech in the House of Commons suggesting that Britain should not adopt the European currency, but that Europe should instead adopt English as its official language.

When Makepeace remonstrates with Urquhart, Urquhart tells him his tenure as Foreign Secretary is over and offers him a new posting. The furious Makepeace resigns from the government, and emerges as the prime minister's main adversary in Parliament.

Ian Richardson, Nickloas Grace, Andrew Seear

THE FINAL CUT EPISODE 3

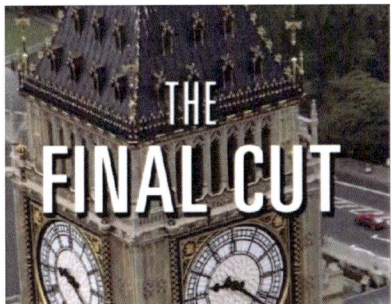

DIRECTED BY Mike Vardy
ORIGINAL AIR DATE: 11/19/95

CAST

Ian Richardson.........Francis Urquhart
Diane Fletcher......Elizabeth Urquhart
Paul Freeman............Tom Makepeace
Isla Blair.......................Claire Carlsen
Nickolas Grace...Geoffrey Booza Pitt
Kevork Malikyan.......................Nures
David Ryall...........Sir Bruce Bullerby
Yolanda Vazquez......Maria Passolides
Cherith Mellor.......Hilary Makepeace
Glyn Grain......................John Rayner
Nick Brimble...........................Corder
Joseph Long............President Nicolau
Duggie Brown...................Joe Badger
Andrew Seear.............Michael Wolfin
Dorothy Vernon......................Speaker
Peter Symonds.......................Polecutt
Boyd Clack...................Hywell Harris
Kate Rickett.....................TV Reporter
Brian Baines........................Chairman
Kenneth Taylor....Florid Backbencher
Susannah Harker............Mattie Storin

Ian Richardson   Diane Fletcher

Paul Freeman   Isla Blair

Nickolas Grace   Kevork Malikyan

David Ryall   Yolanda Vazquez

Michael Fabricant, Roger Grainger, John Lambert................Backbenchers

Cherith Mellor

Glyn Grain

AND: Angela Abrahams, Michael Ackerman, Margaret Alderman, Kitty Aldridge, Jerry Baker, Micky Baker, Mitch Barber, Ann Barrass, Julian Barsham, Paul Barton, Helen Beckman, Lisette Bell-Simmonds, Sacha Bennett, Gerald Benson, Hazel Birrell, Jane Bishop, Judith Blackstad,

Nick Brimble

Joseph Long

George Blee, Jane Bough, Andrew Bowen, Willy Bowman, Raymond Boyd, Mark Brett, Pam Buckley, Ray Burdis, Ron Burrage, Janine Button,

Duggie Brown

Andrew Seear

Roy Byrne, Woolf Byrne, Carol Careford, Giovanni Caruso, Marc Cass, Ray Chaney, Mark Chapman, Nick Chapman, Claire Chrysler, Melita Clarke, Trisha Clarke, John Clements,

Dorothy Vernon

Peter Symonds

Val Clover, Samara Cohen, Freddie Comrie, Ken Coombs, Malcolm Cooper, Lynn Costenbarder, Alan Crisp, Bert Crome, Barry Davey, Cyril Davey, Malcolm Davey, Lionel De Clerc,

Boyd Clack

Kate Rickett

John Denton, Sharton Douglas, Carlos Duque, Chris Dyson, George Ensor, Geoffrey Evans, Susan Farthing, David Field, Joan Field, Neill Finnighan, Juliet Forester, Salo Gardner, Martin Garfield, David Garry, Barry Gay, Andy Gell, Helen Georgette, Selena Gilbert, Anthony Gilding,

Brian Baines

House Dignitary

172

George Gilmour, Laurie Goode, Brian Goodwin, Pat Gorman, Anita Green, Charles Grima, Adrian Hammond, Paul Harris, Cassie Hatton, Tom Hibbert, George Higgins, Dick Hope, Elaine Hopkins, Mex Horne, Ted Houser, Derek Hunt, Philip Ingham, Eric Jack, Jessica James, Juliette James, Leonie Jessel, Dianne Kelly, Michael Kennedy, Mark Kirby, Paul Kirby, Joe Lacey, Penny Lambirth, Pat LeClerc, Aileen Lewis, Alex Lewis, Derek Lyons, Robert McGibbon, Alison McGuire, Steve Marco, Sergio Marini, Colin Martin, Raymond Martin, Tina Maskell, Anna Mattina, Mary Maxted, Erol Mehmet, Richard Moody, Brian Moorehead, Stephen Morphew, Mike Morrell, Mike Mungarvan, Stuart Myers, Ray Nicholas, Clive Norman, Mimi Novic, Gary O'Brien, Kevin O'Brien, Robert Pearson, Andreas Petrides, Philip Phedonos, Carolyn Poole, Theo Pouros, Kaye Power-McGowan, Paul Puig, Celia Radband, Mike Randall, Leslie Rhodes, Ray Riches, Steve Rickard, Denise Ryan, Paul Salt, Simon Sands, Terry Sartain, Daphne Selfe, John Sergent, Molly Seyforth, Carol Shaw, Ted Shepherd, Larry Sheppard, Sally Sinclair, Rodney Smith, Guy Standeven, Douglas Stark, Trevor Steedman, Graham Stevens, Keith Swaden, Joe

M.P. 1   M.P. 2

M.P. 3   M.P. 4

M.P. 5   M.P. 6

Man 1   Man 2

Newsman   Onlooker

Woman

Szucs, Vanessa Taverner, Colin Thomas, Reg Thomason, Mal Tobias, Cy Town, Edwin Ubels, Alan Uttley-Moore, Harry Van Engel, Jennifer Van Engel, Ethel Vawdrey, Paul Vincent, Linn Waldegrave, Leslie Weekes, Howard Whiteson, Kim Whitfield, Eddie Whiting, Alan Wicks, Nick Wilkinson, Tony Winn, Brian Winsor, Peter Zander

Having resigned as Foreign Secretary, Tom Makepeace launches a blistering attack in the House of Commons directed not only at the government in general but at the Prime Minister in particular.

Nickolas Grace, Isla Blair

Outside Number 10

Joseph Long and friends

Nick Brimble, Diane Fletcher, Ian Richardson

Ian Richardson, Isla Blair, Yolanda Vazquez

He then moves across the aisle to sit on the opposition benches. For his part, Francis Urquhart takes it all in stride quite sure of his position and his ability to retain the leadership of the party.

Ian Richardson as Urquhart

Although Claire ends her relationship with Make-peace, she continues to talk to him privately and encourages him to fight Urquhart.

Ian Richardson on the roof

Ian Richardson, Glyn Grain

House of Commons scene

She also advises Maria to take her case to Makepeace, who repeatedly raises the cover-up in Parliament. At Makepeace's suggestion, Claire purloins the original report on the Cyprus killings.

Urquhart doing the crossword puzzle

Ian Richardson, Joseph Long

Diane Fletcher, Kevork Malikyan

The report is obtained with Urquhart's name re-
vealed from the secret government archive where it
is stored, but Urquhart's bodyguard, Corder seizes
the document from her.

Makepeace's leadership challenge has attracted enough support to convince Urquhart that his position is in jeopardy. He decides to leak information regarding the oil deposits in the territory awarded to the Turks in order to stir up a conflict on Cyprus that he can use to unite Britain under his leadership.

Urquhart addresses the House

David Ryall, Nickolas Grace

Ian Richardson, Diane Fletcher

As chance would have it, Cypriot nationalists attack the British High Commission in Cyprus and kidnap the High Commissioner thus allowing Urquhart to question the wisdom of Makepeace's constant challenges on the Cypriot peace deal.

Urquhart wins the next vote over Makepeace by 202 to 140, but he feels that is not enough of a margin for victory, as there was no clear winner.

TV Poster

Yolanda Vazquez, Isla Blair

Nickolas Grace, Ian Richardson

He tells Elizabeth that he will leak information to the Greeks and the French that they have been cynically conned. It will provoke an international incident.

Elizabeth warns that will be very dangerous, but Francis Urquhart does many dangerous things. "This could be our Falklands," Urquhart says.

Ian Richardson, Isla Blair, Nickolas Grace

Nickolas Grace, Ian Richardson, Glyn Grain, Andrew Seear

THE FINAL CUT EPISODE 4

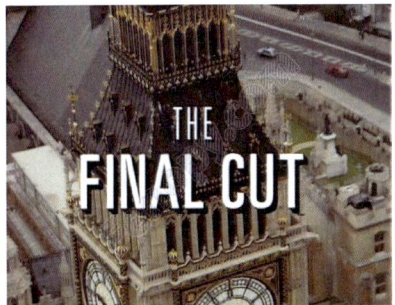

DIRECTED BY Mike Vardy
ORIGINAL AIR DATE: 11/26/95

CAST

Ian Richardson.........Francis Urquhart
Diane Fletcher......Elizabeth Urquhart
Paul Freeman............Tom Makepeace
Isla Blair.......................Claire Carlsen
Nickolas Grace...Geoffrey Booza Pitt
David Henry...............General Gough
John Rowe...............Sir Clive Watling
Glyn Grain.......................John Rayner
Miles Richardson.....Major James Jardine
Yolanda Vazquez......Maria Passolides
Leon Lissek....Evanghelos Passolides
Nick Brimble...........................Corder
Joseph Long..........President Nicolaou
Erika Hoffman.......................Princess
Dorothy Vernon.....................Speaker
Tom Beazley....................Young King
Barry McCarthy...................Grey Suit
Andrew Seear.............Michael Wolfin
Peter Symonds.......................Polecutt
Maria Redmond....................Florence
Richard Bebb................Commentator

Ian Richardson

Diane Fletcher

Paul Freeman

Isla Blair

Nickolas Grace

David Henry

John Rowe

Glyn Grain

David Ashford, Sue Edelson...............
....Newsreaders
Susannah Harker............Mattie Storin
Jessica Gilhooley................Schoolgirl

AND: Angela Abrahams, Michael Ackerman, Margaret Alderman, Kitty Aldridge, Jerry Baker, Micky Baker, Mitch Barber, Ann Barrass, Julian Barsham, Paul Barton, Helen Beckman, Lisette Bell-Simmonds, Sacha Bennett, Gerald Benson, Hazel Birrell, Jane Bishop, Judith Blackstad, George Blee, Jane Bough, Andrew Bowen, Willy Bowman, Raymond Boyd, Mark Brett, Pam Buckley, Ray Burdis, Ron Burrage, Janine Button, Roy Byrne, Woolf Byrne, Carol Careford, Giovanni Caruso, Marc Cass, Ray Chaney, Mark Chapman, Nick Chapman, Claire Chrysler, Melita Clarke, Trisha Clarke, John Clements, Val Clover, Samara Cohen, Freddie Comrie, Ken Coombs, Malcolm Cooper, Lynn Costenbarder, Alan Crisp, Bert Crome, Barry Davey, Cyril Davey, Malcolm Davey, Lionel De Clerc, John Denton, Sharton Douglas, Carlos Duque, Chris Dyson, George Ensor, Geoffrey Evans, Susan Farthing, David Field, Joan Field, Neill Finnighan, Juliet Forester, Salo Gardner, Martin Garfield, David Garry, Barry Gay, Andy Gell, Helen

Miles Richardson

Yolanda Vazquez

Leon Lissek

Nick Brimble

Joseph Long

Barry McCarthy

Andrew Seear

Peter Symonds

Sue Edelson

Dorothy Vernon

Dignitary 1

Dignitary 2

Georgette, Selena Gilbert, Anthony Gilding, George Gilmour, Laurie Goode, Brian Goodwin, Pat Gorman, Anita Green, Charles Grima, Adrian Hammond, Paul Harris, Cassie Hatton, Tom Hibbert, George Higgins, Dick Hope, Elaine Hopkins, Mex Horne, Ted Houser, Derek Hunt, Philip Ingham, Eric Jack, Jessica James, Juliette James, Leonie Jessel, Dianne Kelly, Michael Kennedy, Mark Kirby, Paul Kirby, Joe Lacey, Penny Lambirth, Pat LeClerc, Aileen Lewis, Alex Lewis, Derek Lyons, Robert McGibbon, Alison McGuire, Steve Marco, Sergio Marini, Colin Martin, Raymond Martin, Tina Maskell, Anna Mattina, Mary Maxted, Erol Mehmet, Richard Moody, Brian Moorehead, Stephen Morphew, Mike Morrell, Mike Mungarvan, Stuart Myers, Ray Nicholas, Clive Norman, Mimi Novic, Gary O'Brien, Kevin O'Brien, Robert Pearson, Andreas Petrides, Philip Phedonos, Carolyn Poole, Theo Pouros, Kaye Power-McGowan, Paul

Girl 1   Girl 2

Girl 3   Girl 4

Girl 5   M.P. 1

TV Newsman

Puig, Celia Radband, Mike Randall, Leslie Rhodes, Ray Riches, Steve Rickard, Denise Ryan, Paul Salt, Simon Sands, Terry Sartain, Daphne Selfe, John Sergent, Molly Seyforth, Carol Shaw, Ted Shepherd, Larry Sheppard, Sally Sinclair, Rodney Smith, Guy Standeven, Douglas Stark, Trevor Steedman, Graham Stevens, Keith

Swaden, Joe Szucs, Vanessa Taverner, Colin Thomas, Reg Thomason, Mal Tobias, Cy Town, Edwin Ubels, Alan Uttley-Moore, Harry Van Engel, Jennifer Van Engel, Ethel Vawdrey, Paul Vincent, Linn Waldegrave, Leslie Weekes, Howard Whiteson, Kim Whitfield, Eddie Whiting, Alan Wicks, Nick Wilkinson, Tony Winn, Brian Winsor, Peter Zande

Not having secured enough votes on the first ballot to retain the party leadership, Francis Urquhart plots to not only keep himself in place as Prime Minister, but to win the next general election.

Paul Freeman with security

Clear the roadway!

Ian Richardson as Francis Urquhart

He is desperate to surpass Margaret Thatcher's length of service as PM and decides that to emulate her is likely the best approach: starting a war in Cyprus, his own little Falklands, as he describes it to his wife.

Isla Blair, Nick Brimble

Leon Lissek is shot

It all goes very badly however and the PM's hold on power begins to slip. Claire Coulsen learns that there is a cost to playing both sides in any contest.

Andrew Seear, Glyn Grain, Ian Richardson

Paul Freeman, Isla Blair

Nick Brimble, Paul Freeman

In the end, it's left to Elizabeth Urqhart to come up with a solution that will ensure the PM's legacy for all time. While Urquhart appears defiant, his wife is worried, and she consults Corder for advice on how to save him.

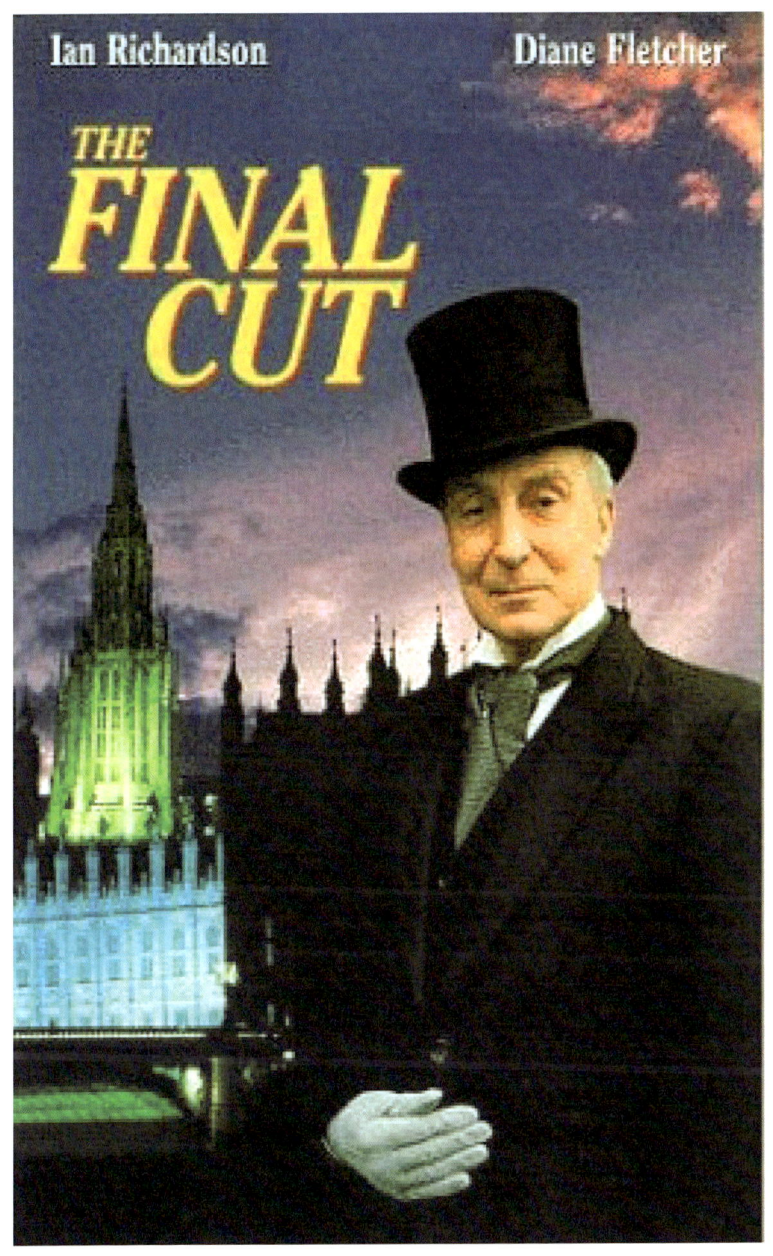

TV Poster

Corder advises "drastic measures, and informs her that he has sent a copy of Mattie Storin's tape, revealing Urquhart's role in her death, to Makepeace. Makepeace confronts the Prime Minister and announces that he will publish the tape, but not before Urquhart has achieved his aim of surpassing Margaret Thatcher's record.

Urquhart looks out the window

David Henry as General Gough

After this, Urquhart again meets Maria. The incriminating Cyprus report has been sent to Maria's father anonymously-presumably by Corder-and Maria vows to publish it.

Boom! Car is a total loss (and also whoever is inside)

Ian Richardson, Nickolas Grace

After this, Urquhart despairs, but Elizabeth tells him they can still be safe and hints at a ploy by Corder. Thing come to a head at the unveiling of the Margaret Thatcher memorial.

John Rowe, Diane Fletcher

Nick Brimble as Corder

Diane Fletcher, Ian Brimble

Glyn Grain, Ian Richardson

On the day when Urquhart surpasses her record, a sniper in Corder's service appears on a rooftop and shoots the prime minister (and Maria's father, who had approached Urquhart with a pistol).

Nicholas Grace, Isla Blair, Andrew Seear, Glyn Grain

Isla Blair, Ian Richardson

Elizabeth had arranged for his assassination as the only way to preserve his reputation (and the retirement fund). Urquhart dies in her arms, while Corder offers his services to Makepeace, the apparent successor.

Sniper on the rooftop

Milton Keynes UK
Ingram Content Group UK Ltd.
UKRC030938230924
448660UK00009B/62